CGP GEOGRAPHY

GCSE GEOGRAPHY

The Essential Workbook

This book covers the GCSE Geography content for the AQA Examining Board, specification A.

Each page of questions covers one page from our AQA A Geography revision guide.

Contents

Published by CGP

Editors:
Kate Houghton
Becky May
Edward Robinson
Rachel Selway

Contributors:
Stephen Buckley, Margaret Collinson,
Chris Kennedy, Barbara Mascetti, Mark Ollis,
Susan Ross, Rebecca Rider, Dennis Watts

With thanks to Edward Robinson and Angela Ryder for proofreading.

The Tectonic Jigsaw

Q1   Copy out the paragraph below using the right words.

> (**Plates / Tectonics**) float on the surface of the earth.
> They move slowly apart from, towards or beside each other
> due to (**convection / sea**) currents. At the edges, plates meet
> at (**folds / boundaries**) or plate (**mountains / margins**).

Q2   Copy and complete the table below.

	Direction plates are moving	Type of boundary	Example

Q3   Are the statements below about tectonic plates true or false?

a)   North and South America both share the same plate.

b)   The Eurasian and Pacific plates are moving towards each other.

c)   Earthquakes and volcanoes are never found at the edges of plates.

d)   The Nazca plate is found to the east of the South American Plate.

Q4   Match up the types of tectonic activity with the plate margin where they might be found.

Tectonic activity:	Plate margin:
Volcanoes	Tensional
Earthquakes	Compressional
Fold mountains, earthquakes and volcanoes	Transform

Earthquakes

Q1 **Three statements about how an earthquake happens are jumbled up below.**
Copy them down in the right order.

- Movement is quick and sudden, creating seismic waves.
- Pressure eventually builds up so much that it can overcome friction.
- At plate boundaries, friction between the plates stops them sliding.

Q2 **Match up the key terms to their definitions.**

Focus   A system used to measure the size of earthquakes.

Epicentre   An instrument which detects vibrations.

Richter scale   The point above the focus, where the effect is strongest.

Seismometer   The point, usually below the surface of the earth,
                             where the plates touch and an earthquake starts.

Q3 **Look at the diagram below and then answer the questions.**

The Richter Scale and Possible Effects

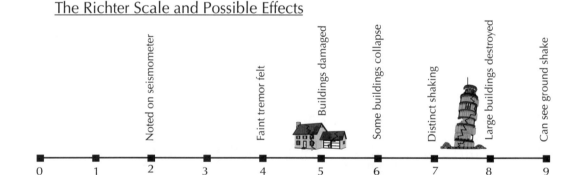

a) Earthquakes are first felt at a Richter scale value of _____ .

b) If the Eiffel Tower were to collapse in an earthquake, what would be the minimum Richter scale value of the earthquake?

c) A logarithmic scale means that a value of 6 is _____ times larger than a value of 5.

Q4 **In May 2003 an earthquake of 6.8 was recorded in Algeria.**
Using the Richter scale diagram above, list the likely effects.

Q1   Write a definition for each of the three volcano-related words below.

   a)   Extinct

   b)   Dormant

   c)   Active

Q2   Copy and complete the crossword below.

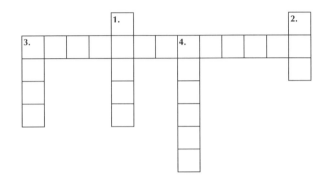

   1 down   Underground molten rock.

   2 down   Fine dust which settles all over the surroundings.

   3 across   Hard solid rock projectiles fired into the air.

   3 down   The main tube lava travels up to reach the surface.

   4 down   Dish-like opening at the top of a volcano.

Q3   Copy the table and fit the sketches, materials and examples into the right places.

Sketches:

Materials: Runny, basic lava   Lava and ash   Thick, acid lava
Examples: Mauna Loa, Hawaii   Mt. Etna   Mt. St. Helens

	Shield	Dome	Composite
Sketch			
Made from			
Example			

Fold Mountains

Q1 Copy out the paragraph below using the correct words.

As two **(tectonic / volcanic)** plates move towards each other, they are said to **(jump / collide)**. The **(water / rock)** between these two plates is pushed up, buckling and turning into **(mountains / glaciers)**. These **(mountain / valley)** ranges are often very **(high / low)** with **(gentle / steep)** slopes.

Q2 The European Alps are an example of a fold mountain range.
Draw a rough copy of the map of Europe below, and mark on the European Alps.

Q3 People who live in mountainous areas use the landscape to their advantage.
Match the following activities to the landscape features which make them effective.

Activities:	**Features:**
Farming	Slopes on which conifers, but not crops, grow well.
Tourism	Flat valleys with deep soil between mountains.
Forestry	Steep-sided mountains with fast-flowing rivers.
Hydro-electric power	Spectacular scenery and good skiing conditions.

Q4 Give examples of each of the following products of the Alps.

a) Crops grown in the Alps

b) Winter sports popular in the Alps

c) Uses of the conifers grown on the slopes of the Alps

Q1   **Copy out the paragraph below, filling in the spaces with the correct words.**

Many people live in areas where volcanoes and earthquakes are common,
even though it's _____ . There are a number of reasons:

- Volcanic lava and ash make _____ _____ which are good for farming.

- Precious _____ and fossil _____ are found nearby.

- Land is less favourable which makes it _____ , so poorer people can
  afford to live there.

- Modern technology means that earthquakes can be _____ ,
  so people will have a chance to prepare for them and won't be taken by surprise.

Q2   **How might monitoring the things below help predict future hazards?**

a)   Wells

b)   Magma temperature

c)   Animal behaviour

d)   Volcano sides

Q3   **Different groups of people have different opinions about living in tectonic areas.
Match up the people below with the opinion that they're most likely to express.**

Local farmer   "We can't be held responsible if people stay voluntarily."
Government official   "People can live there if they want. I can give them employment."
Voluntary aid worker   "I refuse to move — this is my home."
Fossil fuel trader   "It's a foolish risk that wastes so much human life."

Q4   **Living near tectonic activity can be dangerous, but there are some benefits.
Decide whether the advantages below are true or false.**

a)   Crops grow quickly and have high yields.

b)   Some of the gases released have important health benefits.

c)   Geothermal energy can be used to generate electricity.

d)   Hot springs can be used for heating and hot water.

Surviving Tectonic Hazards

Q1 Tectonic hazards have different effects in different places.
For each pair below, decide which would suffer the most serious effects in an earthquake.
For each one, write a sentence explaining your choice.

   a)   Urban location / rural location

   b)   Area of low population density / Area of high population density

   c)   LEDC / MEDC

Q2 When disasters happen lots of things need to be done, so rescue organisers need to prioritise their efforts. Copy out the table and then fit the words below into the correct places.

Immediate	Short-term

First aid   Food aid

Power supply   Putting out fires

Searching for injured   Water supply

Q3 LEDCs are often less able to deal with emergencies than MEDCs.
Link each fact about LEDCs with the appropriate consequence to complete each sentence.

Not many maps or street plans are available...   ... so fires spread quickly.

Houses are poorly made and close together...   ... so it's difficult to co-ordinate rescues.

Medicine is limited...   ... so it's difficult to treat injuries.

Emergencies aren't well predicted...   ... so the government is unprepared.

There are poor communications...   ... so it's hard to get aid to the right places.

Q4 Look carefully at the data about the recent earthquakes in Japan and Algeria.

	Honshu Island, Japan	Algeria
Date	26 May 2003	21 May 2003
Depth of focus	68 km	10 km
No. killed	0	2000
No. injured	104	9085
Other effects	some landslides	200 000 homeless

The Algerian earthquake had more devastating effects than the Japanese earthquake.
Give two reasons why this is so.

Q1 Write a definition for each of the types of rock below.

    a) Igneous

    b) Sedimentary

    c) Metamorphic

Q2 Copy and complete the table about igneous rocks below, by choosing the correct words and phrases from the box.

batholiths and tors	at surface	fine	below surface
dolerite	basalt	coarse	hexagonal columns

	Extrusive	Intrusive
Texture		
Method of cooling		
Features		
Example		

Q3 Give brief answers to these questions:

    a) What are chalk and limestone made from?

    b) What is coal made from?

    c) Sandstone, clays and shales are found in layers.
       What are these layers called?

    d) What do you call the horizontal layers of rock where magma has
       been forced along bedding planes?

    e) What shape are the giant basalt columns found on the Giant's Causeway in Ireland?

Q4 Copy the boxes and arrows and fill in the blanks to show how metamorphic rocks change.

Clays become [ ]   [ ] becomes **Quartzite**

[ ] becomes **Gneiss**   **Limestone** becomes [ ]

Weathering and Quarrying

Q1   **Freeze-thaw weathering is common in temperate climates such as the British Isles.
Put the sentences below in the right order to show the process of freeze-thaw weathering.**

1. During the day, the ice melts, contracts and releases the pressure on the rock.

2. Pieces of rock break off (frost shattering), producing scree at the foot of steep slopes.

3. This alternating expansion and contraction weakens the rock.

4. Water gets trapped in the cracks in rocks.

5. When the temperature drops at night, the water freezes, expands and puts pressure
   on the rock sides.

Q2   **Copy out the sentences filling in the correct words.**

Carbonic acid is made from limestone and _____ water.

Caves, swallow holes, clints and grykes are all called _____ features —

they are formed when the rock _____ along weaknesses like joints.

The dissolved rock drips onto cave roofs and floors forming _____

and _____.

Q3   **Use the correct names from the diagram to complete the crossword.**

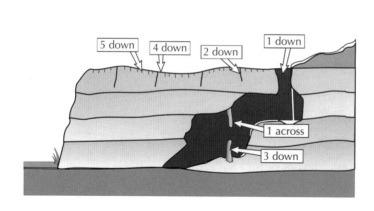

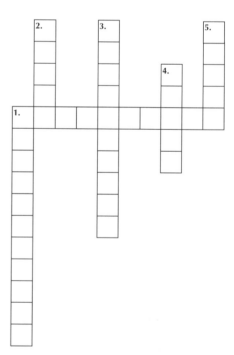

Q4   **There are both advantages and disadvantages to quarries. Decide if a quarry would be
a good or a bad thing for each topic below, and write a short sentence to explain why.**

a) Building materials   b) Employment   c) Tourism   d) Traffic   e) Environment

Rocks, Landscapes and People

Q1   Make three columns headed Granite, Limestone and Chalk.
Copy the facts below under the correct headings (there are four of each).

Very resistant to erosion.

Can be used as a natural reservoir.

Forms flat-topped moorlands with steep gorges.

Impermeable, so water stays on the surface, creating marshes.

Also known as karst scenery.

Forms escarpments or cuestas.

Dartmoor has this type of rock.

Quarried for lime, cement and building blocks.

The Yorkshire Dales has this type of rock.

Soil is infertile and unsuitable for farming.

The South Downs has this type of rock.

Soil is suitable for sheep farming and cereal crops.

Q2   Copy and label the diagram of a chalk escarpment below.

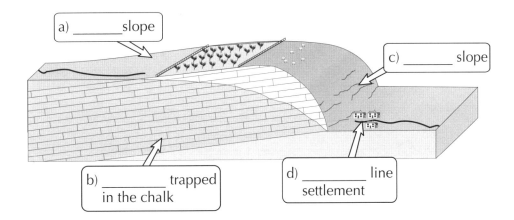

a) _____ slope

c) _____ slope

b) _____ trapped
in the chalk

d) _____ line
settlement

Q3   Match together the beginnings of the sentences below with their correct endings.

Clay forms vales, which are...

Clay is impermeable, which means...

Clay soil is unsuitable for...

Clay can be dug up for...

Clay vales are often used for...

...making bricks.

...arable farming.

...wide areas of flat lowland.

...pasture.

...water can't soak through.

Rivers and Valleys

Q1 Copy out the table below, choosing the correct terms to describe the stages of a river's flow.

	Width	Discharge
Source	narrow / wide	high / low
Mouth	narrow / wide	high / low

Q2 Answer the questions below with a short phrase or word.

a) When might a river have high energy levels?

b) Give the term for the material produced when rivers erode the bank and beds.

c) When a river has little energy to carry material, what process occurs?

Q3 Copy and complete the table to describe the three stages of a river valley cross profile.

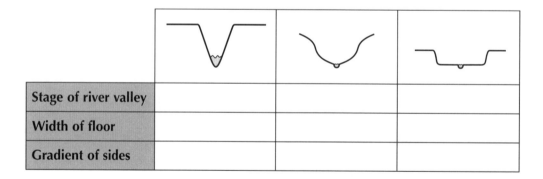

Stage of river valley			
Width of floor			
Gradient of sides			

Q4 Give a brief description of each of the erosion processes named below.

a) Attrition.

b) Corrasion.

c) Solution.

d) Hydraulic action.

Erosion, Transportation and Deposition

Q1 Copy and complete the table below showing the three types of river erosion.

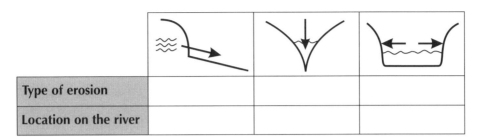

Type of erosion			
Location on the river			

Q2 The diagrams below show four different ways a river can transport its load. Complete the crossword using the proper names of each type of transport.

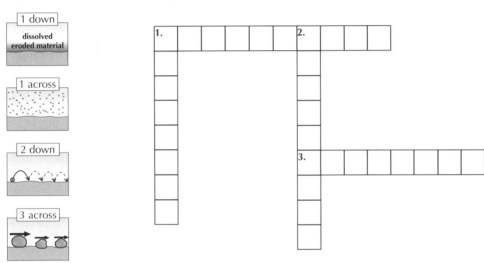

Q3 Copy out the passage and fill in the missing words using words from the box.

velocity	load	material	landslide	deltas

Deposition happens when a river's _____ is much lower than normal. It loses energy and is unable to carry the _____ and so drops it on the beds and bank. Likewise if there is an increase in the _____ carried by the river, it will deposit its load. This often happens after a _____ or glaciation. Deposition can cause landforms called _____ when rivers enter lakes or the sea.

Q4 Copy out the sentences below in the right order to show the four stages of deposition.

1. Gravel, sand and silt carried as bedload or in suspension are deposited in lower stages.

2. Large material is deposited in the river's higher stages.

3. Dissolved material is carried out to sea.

4. Suspended silt and clay are carried out into estuaries and deltas.

River Features of the Upper Stage

Q1 Copy out the sentences inserting the correct words from the box in the right places.

> twists and turns   vertically   uphill   downhill   laterally

    a) Because it starts off high in the mountains, the river flows _____ to reach the sea.

    b) The river erodes _____ in its upper stage.

    c) Interlocking spurs mean the river _____ down the valley.

Q2 Use the diagrams below to write a short paragraph about what happens when a waterfall is formed.

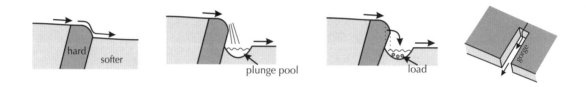

Q3 Copy the river bed shape below.
Add bands of hard and soft rock to show how it became this shape.

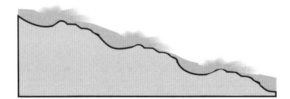

Q4 Copy out the sentences below using the correct choice of words.

    a) Rapids are **(larger / smaller)** than waterfalls.

    b) Rapids and waterfalls are found in the **(upper / lower / middle)** stage of a river.

Q5 Below are two places whose names give a clue as to what you might find there.
One has a waterfall the other has rapids. Which is which?

The White Water Hotel on the River Leven

Thornton Force in the Yorkshire Dales

River Features of Middle & Lower Stages

Q1 Look at the diagram which shows a cross-section of a river meander.
Then copy the table and fit the words from below in the right place.

fast   slow   shallow   deep   cliff   beach   deposition   erosion

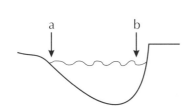

	a	b
speed		
depth		
process		
landform		

Q2 Use the four diagrams below to explain the stages in the formation of an oxbow lake.

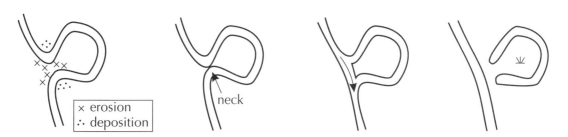

x erosion
∴ deposition

neck

Q3 The following sentences describe features of the lower stage of a river.
Name the feature that each sentence describes.

a) Material deposited by a river, usually very fertile.

b) Landform caused by too much load or tide insufficient to carry it away.

c) Funnel-shaped river mouth.

d) Raised river banks made from coarse deposited alluvium.

e) Flat, wide valley floor that's able to accommodate flood water.

Q4 Copy the table below and fill in the correct words in the right places.

	Type	Characteristics	Example
Mediterranean Sea		angular / rounded few / many tributaries	
Mediterranean Sea		even / uneven spread of deposition many / few tributaries	
Gulf of Mexico		few / many main tributaries short / stretches out to sea	

River Features on Maps

Q1   Find the River Esk and Glenderaterra Beck on the map extracts.
Which is an upland river and which is a lowland river? How can you tell?

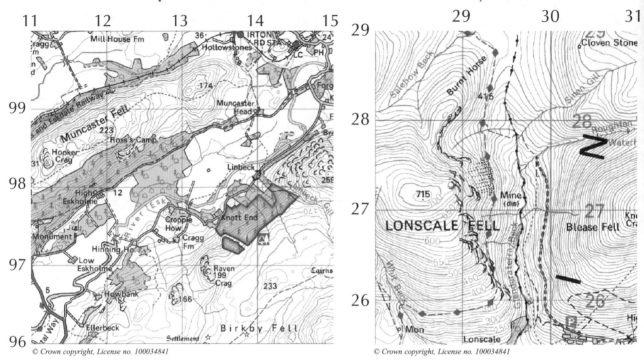

© Crown copyright, License no. 100034841   © Crown copyright, License no. 100034841

Q2   The following questions are about the Muncaster Fell map extract.

a)   What do you call the river feature at 115967?

b)   What is the river landform at 133977?

c)   Water, which falls on Raven Crag (134969) and flows down towards
Cropple How, reaches the river much quicker than water falling at
140974 and flowing towards Knott End. Why is this?

Q3   All of the questions below are about the Lonscale Fell map extract.
Glenderaterra Beck flows from Skiddaw Forest, which is no longer covered in
trees. The forest is on one of the three highest mountains in the Lake District.

a)   Roughton Gill has two waterfalls. Give their six figure grid references.

b)   In square 2927 there is lots of evidence that weathering is taking
place as the river erodes laterally. What landform indicates this?

c)   What evidence is there in square 2927 that as the river bed has
eroded downwards it has exposed valuable rock?

Q1 Copy and complete the table below, choosing the option which makes flooding more likely.

Factor	State when flooding most likely
Total rainfall	high / low
Intensity of rain	high / low
Wetness of ground	saturated / dry
Rock type	porous / impermeable
Ground cover	vegetated / bare
Slope angle	steep / gentle

Q2 Copy out the passage below, filling in the missing words.

As well as physical causes of flooding, there are also _____ causes: _____ means that there are more buildings and concrete surfaces. This leads to less infiltration and more surface _____. Water can also get to rivers very quickly through _____.

_____ is where large areas of trees are chopped down for wood and farmland. It reduces _____ and _____, so more water will eventually reach the river and the risk of flooding will be increased.

Q3 Match the types of flood damage below with the longer-term problems caused.

Damaged buildings

Damaged farmland

Damaged transport and communication systems

Power supplies cut off

Aid relief hindered

Rebuilding work hindered

Homelessness

Reduced economic output

Managing Flooding

Q1 **Match the beginnings of the sentences below with their correct endings.**

Short-term responses...   ...can be used to prevent further damage to properties.

Emergency responses in a flood...   ...is known as evacuation.

People being moved to safer areas...   ...can save lives and prevent further damage.

Sandbags...   ...are also known as emergency responses.

Q2 **Below are four diagrams showing how engineers have changed the shapes of rivers to combat flooding. Look at each one carefully and then explain how it is used to manage flooding.**

a)

River Rhine

b)

River Yangtze

c)

Los Angeles

d)
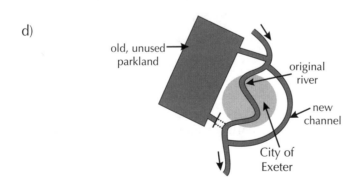
old, unused parkland
original river
new channel
City of Exeter

Q3 **Long-term solutions such as dams and reservoirs bring both advantages and disadvantages. Draw a table with two columns to list the good and bad points (at least three of each).**

Q1 Describe in one sentence how soft engineering is different from hard engineering.

Q2 Complete the paragraph below by filling in the missing words.

_____ engineering means building major structures like dams and
canals to prevent flooding. There are a number of disadvantages:
Channels need to be _____ or they will eventually fill up with
deposits, becoming smaller and less effective at preventing _____.
Water flows _____ in new channels, which can increase flooding
and _____ further downstream. If a dam or cut-through collapses,
there can be a huge, sudden disaster.

Q3 Use the clues to solve the crossword. All the answers relate to hard or soft engineering.

1 across   scheme which reduces run-off as trees intercept the rain
2 down   leaving land up-river as _____ gives continuous plant cover
3 across   impermeable man made surface good for roads, bad for floods
4 across   using past data to look into the future
5 down   preferable to concrete
6 down   moving water to more appropriate places
7 across   ways of stopping flooding
8 down   countries which are lagging behind with soft engineering
9 across   Sustainable Urban Drainage Systems

Glacial Erosion

Q1 **Some of the statements below are true and some are false.**
Copy out the true statements.

A corrie is a hollow where a glacier starts.

A corrie has a steep back wall.

The back of a corrie is formed by deposition.

A Bergschrund is a type of dog that pulls sledges over glaciers.

An arête is a steep-sided knife-edged ridge.

A pyramidal peak is found where several corries meet around a mountain summit.

There are many glacier-formed pyramidal peaks near the River Nile in Egypt.

Q2 **Look at the diagram below of a glaciated highland landscape.**

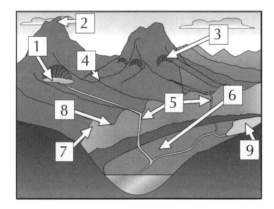

a) Match each number on the diagram with one of the following terms:

Arête	**Ribbon lake**	**Corrie**
Waterfalls	**Pyramidal peak**	**Corrie lake (tarn)**
Hanging valley	**Flood plain**	**Truncated spur**

b) Explain how this valley was altered and shaped by a glacier. Your description should include an explanation of how the following features arose:

    truncated spurs   **hanging valleys**   **ribbon lakes**

Q3 **Copy out the following sentences with their correct endings:**

A ribbon lake is...   ...formed high up in a corrie.

A tarn is...   ...smooth on one side and rough on the other.

Waterfalls are...   ...long and narrow and on the floor of a glaciated valley.

Roche moutonnees are...   ...often found at the lower end of a hanging valley.

Q1   Glaciers eventually drop their load of eroded material when they melt and
retreat. Match the terms listed below to the descriptions of different deposits.

terminal moraine   **erratics**   **drumlins**

ground moraine   **lateral moraine**

a)   Pieces of rock moved by a glacier and dropped on a different rock type.

b)   Rock material laid down by a melting and retreating glacier along the
sides of the valley.

c)   Long narrow hills which are usually round and steeply sloping at the
upstream end and pointed and gently sloping at the downstream end.

d)   Piles of stones, boulders and clays on the floor of the valley.

e)   Rock material deposited at the end of the glacier.

Q2   The diagram below shows the junction of two glaciers.
Decide which type of moraines are found at A, B, C and D.

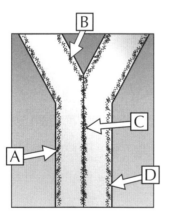

Q3   Copy and complete the following sentences by choosing the correct words.

a)   **(Drumlins / erratics)** often occur in groups called 'baskets of eggs'.

b)   Drumlins are more round and blunt at the **(upstream / downstream)** end.

c)   Ground moraines are also called **(erratics / till)**.

d)   Ground moraines are **(organised / disorganised)** piles of rocks with
(no / a) distinctive shape.

Glacial Features on Maps

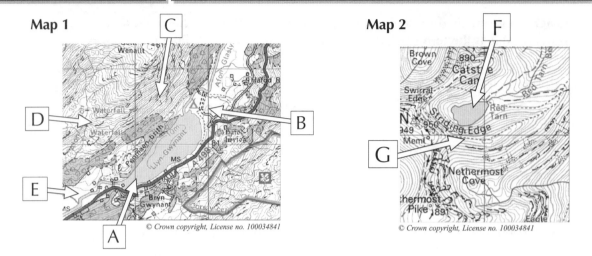

Map 1

C

D

E

A

B

© Crown copyright, License no. 100034841

Map 2

F

G

© Crown copyright, License no. 100034841

Q1 **On map 1 above, there are features labelled A to E.**
Match each feature to one of the terms below.

> **ribbon lake**   **hanging valley**   **flat valley floor**
>
> **steep valley side**   **roche moutonnée or drumlin.**

Q2 **Answer the following questions about map 1.**

     a)   Explain why it is difficult to tell from the map whether one of the features is a roche moutonnée or a drumlin.

     b)   Describe the overall shape and appearance of the main valley on the map.

     c)   Where is the campsite? What features make this a good location for it?

     d)   Suggest one reason why most of the housing is clustered on the valley floor.

Q3 **On map 2 there are features labelled F and G.**

     a)   Name the type of lake labelled F.

     b)   What is the word for the hollow that lake F is in?

     c)   Which of the following terms is often used to describe the hollow?

        plate shaped, armchair shaped, dome shaped, bucket shaped

     d)   What word is normally used for the type of feature found at G?

Q1   The extract below was written to encourage tourists to visit the Lake District.
Copy each of the underlined phrases and give the proper geographical term
for each feature described.

Part of a tourist guide about the Lake District:

The <u>deep valleys have steep sides</u> that lead up to magnificent
mountains. The <u>long, narrow lakes</u> in many of the valleys
reflect superb <u>mountain peaks</u>. These lakes are ideal for
sailing and canoeing. Roads through the valleys wind round
<u>rocky outcrops</u> where sheep graze.

The high and rugged <u>sharp ridges</u> are a challenge for the more energetic and well-equipped
walkers. They are well-rewarded with magnificent views over <u>small lakes hidden in hollows</u>
in the high mountainsides. Streams suddenly plunge down from <u>higher valleys</u> into the
deeper lake-filled valleys, making beautiful waterfalls.

Q2   Answer the questions below on farming in glaciated areas.

a)   What types of farming can be done in glaciated highland areas like the Lake District?
In which parts of the valley is each type mainly done?

b)   What have glaciers done that has made the growing of crops difficult or impossible?

c)   What alternative sources of income can farmers exploit in this difficult environment?

d)   How has glacial deposition helped farmers in lowland areas like East Anglia?

Q3   Copy and complete the following passage.

In some upland glaciated areas, the land is too _____ to grow crops on.
Farmers have often diversified in these areas by planting _____ trees,
which can _____ in the cold, wet and windy conditions of upland
glaciated areas. The forests have often become a _____ attraction as
well as helping the farmers make _____ through commercial forestry.

Q4   What does HEP stand for, and why are glaciated highlands suitable for it?

Managing Glacial Landscapes

Q1 Conflicts occur in glaciated mountain areas as they can be used in many different ways. Explain why conflict might arise between the following groups:

    a) Water companies versus farmers.

    b) Conservationists versus tourists.

    c) Farmers versus road builders and developers.

    d) Speedboat owners versus conservationists.

Q2 What role do National Park Authorities have to play in solving the issues described in Q1?

Q3 Copy the sentences below, choosing the correct word from each pair.

    a) Tourists are (**good / bad**) for the economy of an area.

    b) Tourism is often (**discouraged / encouraged**) for financial reasons.

    c) Tourists in the Lake District have led to environmental (**problems / benefits**) such as footpath (**conservation / erosion**).

    d) So that tourism can continue with little environmental impact, it should be (**subsistent / sustainable**).

Q4 Write down the terms that the following sentences are definitions of.

    a) Meeting the needs of today's population without harming the ability of future generations to meet their own needs.

    b) Where farmers develop other business activities like rare breed centres in addition to traditional ones.

    c) Areas of outstanding natural beauty, which are managed so that they can be preserved for future generations.

    d) The destruction of the natural environment through noise, pollution, litter, erosion or development, for example.

Q1 Draw two columns and write the headings 'constructive waves' and 'destructive waves' at the top. Then write each of the following phrases in the correct column:

> Cause a lot of erosion.
>
> Cause more deposition than erosion.
>
> Operate in calm weather.
>
> Operate in storm conditions.
>
> The swash is strong.
>
> The backwash is strong.
>
> Are often about 5 or 6 metres high.
>
> Are about one metre high.

Q2 Unscramble the words below to find five ways that the sea erodes the coast. Then explain how each process works.

> a) crudyhila nicota
>
> b) weav pignound
>
> c) norattiti
>
> d) racoonsir
>
> e) noisrocro

Q3 Look at the diagram below and answer the questions.

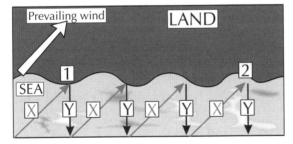

> a) What is it called when the wind makes waves break at an oblique angle to the shore?
>
> b) Copy the diagram and write a key for it, to show what the letters X and Y stand for.
>
> c) Explain how a stone from point 1 is moved along the beach to point 2 by this process.

Q4 Name the four ways in which waves transport material, and briefly describe how each one works.

Coastal Landforms from Erosion

This is a picture of part of a village threatened by erosion on the Holderness coastline in Yorkshire.

Q1 The cliff below this small group of houses is being undercut by wave erosion.
The sea erodes three quarters of a metre of cliff each year.
It is cheaper to re-house the people who live there than to try to stop the erosion.

   a) What are the four processes of erosion that have made the steep cliffs and now threaten to cause the village to collapse into the sea?

   b) Explain how the waves erode the cliff. Include the following words in your explanation: notch, unstable, collapse, retreat.

Q2 Complete this sentence by adding the correct ending from the list below:
The sea erodes mainly...

   a) ... on the sea bed.

   b) ... between high and low tide levels.

   c) ... above sea level.

   d) ... in dredged channels.

Q3 Draw a simple plan view diagram to show how alternate hard and soft bands of rock can affect the shape of the coast. Label the diagram to show what happens.

Q4 Off the coast of Dorset, near Swanage, there are Old Harry and Old Harry's Wife —
two tall pillars of rock that look like very small islands.
Which of the following words is a term for this type of landform caused by erosion?

   towers   **strandeds**   **tall pillars**   **stacks**

Q5 Copy the diagram below and complete it by correctly labelling the erosional features.

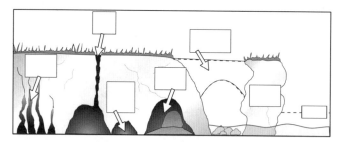

Coastal Landforms from Deposition

Q1 Waves erode the coast but whatever they pick up, they have to eventually drop again. **This is called deposition and it is how beaches and some coastal landforms are made.**

Look at the diagram on the right and answer the questions below.

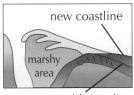

a) What is the name of the coastal feature shown in the diagram?

b) Draw three diagrams to show how the feature in the diagram was formed, stage by stage, by longshore drift. Add labels to your three diagrams.

c) Describe the formation of salt marshes behind such features.

Q2 **Describe each of the following and explain how they are formed by deposition:**

a) Tombolo

b) Barrier beach

c) Mud flats

d) Storm beach

Q3 Explain how a barrier beach differs from a spit.

Q4 Waves have the energy to move material which was previously eroded.
Copy out the following sentences, choosing the correct words where there is a choice.

a) The more energy a wave has, the **(bigger / smaller)** the rock fragments it can move.

b) Large rocks are likely to be piled at the top of a beach by **(low / high)** energy waves.

c) A lagoon is trapped and **(exposed to / protected from)** the energy of waves.

d) **(Mud flats /Stacks)** often form in river estuaries.

Q5 Longshore drift causes most depositional features on the coast to form and grow gradually bigger. Suggest what might happen to depositional features when barriers such as groynes or a harbour breakwater are constructed and cut off the supply of eroded material.

Coastal Features on Maps

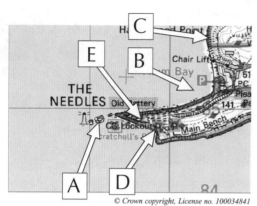

Map 2

Map 1

THE NEEDLES

© Crown copyright, License no. 100034841   © Crown copyright, License no. 100034841

Q1   **Look at map 1 which shows the Needles on the Isle of Wight.**
Match the features listed below to the letters on the map where they can be found.

Headland made of hard rock, difficult for waves to erode.

Bay eroded into soft, easily eroded rock.

Stacks separated from land by erosion.

Cliff eroded by waves.

Wave cut platform.

Q2   **Below are words and names that may appear on a map near the coast.**
Choose and write the words and names that help to indicate a cliff is nearby.

Cliff Top House	**Lookout**	**Marshland**	**Viewpoint**	**Estuary**
Lovers' Leap	**Mud flat**	**Country park**	**Steep End**	**Caves**

Q3   **Answer the questions below about map 2, which shows Hurst Spit on the south coast.**

a)   On the map, what evidence is there that coastal erosion and
longshore drift occur and have been a problem for the town?

b)   Describe the shape of the spit. Give an explanation of
how it was formed, using evidence from the map.

c)   How can you tell from the map that Hurst Spit is a <u>mature</u> spit?

d)   List the ways humans have affected the coastal environment on the map.

The map extract below shows part of the Isle of Wight. The area includes a length of coast visited by many people. The letters indicate features which attract visitors and areas affected by visitors.

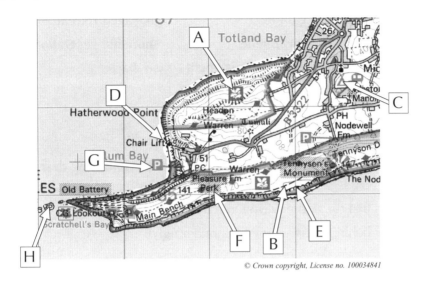

© Crown copyright, License no. 100034841

Q1 Look at the map above. Match the features listed below to the letters on the map where they can be found.

Stacks

Steep cliffs

Footpath where erosion may occur

Area preserved by National Trust

Car park provided for access

Facility to provide access and reduce erosion

Campsite located to avoid spoiling coastal views

Facility that conservationists might object to

Q2 Answer the questions below about how people cause coastal erosion.

a) For many years, people were allowed to remove coloured sands from the cliffs at Alum Bay to put into glass tubes as souvenirs. What effect do you think this has had on the cliffs?

b) How can erosion caused by people walking be reduced?

Q3 What do local and national governments have to consider when managing areas of coast like the area in the map?

Flood and Erosion Control

Q1 Make two columns with the headings 'hard engineering' and 'soft engineering'.
Then list the flood and erosion control methods from below in their correct columns.

sea walls	gabions	managed retreat
armoured blocks	revetments	shoreline vegetation
dune stabilisation	beach nourishment	set backs

Q2 From the lists you have made, choose a term for each of the following descriptions:

a) Slatted barriers that break the wave force by trapping beach material behind them. They look rather ugly.

b) Instead of spending more and more money on protecting the coast, the sea is allowed to flood into parts of low lying areas.

c) Steel mesh cages full of rocks that absorb some of the wave energy and slow down erosion.

d) Planting of vegetation so that the roots of the plants will hold the beach sediment together.

e) Big mounds of sand are kept in place by planting marram grass and by keeping people to particular footpaths.

Q3 Look at the diagram below of a type of hard engineering coastal defence.

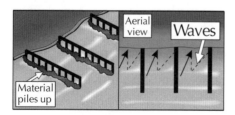

a) What type of coastal defence does this diagram show?

b) Explain how the structures in the diagram can help to protect the coast.

Q4 Why is it often better, and more sustainable, to use soft engineering rather than hard engineering to protect the coast?

World Climate Zones

Q1 The map below shows the climate zones for part of the world, eight of which are labelled. Match the climate zones from the list with their correct letters on the map.

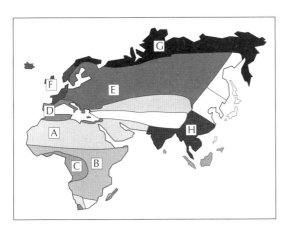

Mediterranean

Equatorial

Deserts

Continental

Mid-latitude west coast

Tundra

Tropical Monsoon

Tropical wet summer

Q2 Which four climatic zones from the list above are made warmest by being near to the Equator?

Q3 The overall temperature decreases and the temperature range increases as you get further from the equator. Explain why.

Q4 Copy and complete the sentences below by choosing the correct word from each pair:

a) Temperature usually **(increases / decreases)** as you go higher up mountains.

b) There is usually **(more / less)** rainfall on high ground than on lower ground.

c) Coastal areas have a **(smaller / larger)** temperature range than those further inland.

Q5 Match up the parts of each sentence below to make four complete statements.

Prevailing winds blowing from hot areas...   ...bring rain.

Prevailing winds blowing from colder areas...   ...raise temperatures.

Prevailing winds blowing from the sea...   ...reduce rainfall.

Prevailing winds blowing from dry land...   ...lower temperatures.

Q6 Look at the climatic figures for a country in the table below. Decide which climatic zone the country is located within and explain how you know.

Months	J	F	M	A	M	J	J	A	S	O	N	D
Rainfall (mm)	350	340	370	380	375	380	370	375	385	400	390	400
Temperature (°C)	28	29	28	30	28	29	29	28	30	30	29	28

29

Precipitation and the UK Climate

Q1 Look at the diagram of relief rainfall below.
Then match the words listed below to the correct letter on the diagram.

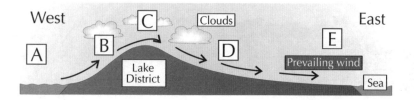

West   [C]   Clouds   East

[A]   [B]   [D]   [E]

Lake District   Prevailing wind   Sea

drier air   **warm, wet onshore winds**   **air rises and cools**

rain shadow area   **water vapour condenses**

Q2 Copy the sentences below, choosing the correct word from each pair provided:

a) Relief rain falls when warm, wet onshore winds reach a **(mountain / coastal)** barrier.

b) Precipitation caused by warm air rising is called **(conventional / convectional)** rain.

c) Precipitation occurs when water vapour **(cools / warms)**.

d) The air becomes **(saturated / scorched)** at the **(dew / rain)** point.

e) Tiny water droplets form and join together, leading to **(convection / precipitation)**.

Q3 State which of the sentences below are true and which are false.
Then write a correction for the false statements.

a) In hot equatorial areas, convectional rainfall occurs all year round.

b) Heated air spreads out on the Earth's surface and causes rain.

c) Thunder and lightning are caused by clouds hitting each other.

d) Convectional rain occurs in the UK when temperatures are high.

e) Thermal up-currents cause low air pressure.

Q4 Which of the following statements explains how frontal rain occurs?

Thunder and lightning break through a cloud.

Warm and cold air meet at a front.

Warm onshore winds reach a mountain barrier and rise over it.

An anticyclone becomes established.

Q5 Name and describe the UK's climate type.

Q1 The UK's very changeable weather is mainly caused by low pressure systems.
Copy out this passage choosing the correct word from each pair.

(**Warm / Cold**) and wet tropical maritime air from the (**south / north**) meets

(**warm / cold**) polar air from the (**north / south**) over the Atlantic Ocean in the

(**east / west**) of the UK. Because warm air rises over colder air, (**high / low**) air pressure

is created. Where air of different temperatures meet, (**fronts / backs**) are formed.

These move over the UK and bring (**sunshine / rain**) along with changes in temperature.

Q2 What weather system would be ideal for a sports day
— high pressure or low pressure? Explain your answer.

Q3 The diagram below shows a cross section through part of a depression.

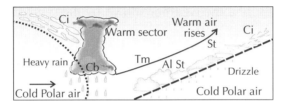

a) Choose the correct meanings from the choices below to make a key for the diagram.

Tm	(time meter / tropical maritime / top most)
Cb	(columbusnimbus / comnibusnimbus / cumulonimbus)
Ci	(cirrus / curris / cissus)
St	(storm / status / stratus)
Al St	(albert stratus / altostratus / altar starus)
_ _ _ _(dashed line)	(cold front / warm front / occluded front)
. . . . . .(dotted line)	(cold front / warm front / occluded front)

b) What weather would you experience as a depression passes over you?

Q4 Make two columns with the headings 'Anticyclonic weather in summer' and 'Anticyclonic
weather in winter'. Then copy the words and phrases below into the correct columns.

Very dry, hot weather   Heat wave

Little heat lost during short night   Freezing fog

Sometimes below freezing all day   Heat lost by radiation during long night

Frost   25°C or higher

Q5 Are the following sentences true or false?

a) Stable conditions occur in low pressure systems.

b) Temperature inversions often cause fog.

c) Skies are usually clear in anticyclones.

Synoptic Charts

Q1   Copy out the following sentences choosing the correct words or phrases.

   a)   A synoptic chart is a **(weather map / rainfall graph)**.

   b)   A westerly wind blows **(from / to)** the west.

   c)   The weather station symbols on a chart show **(weather / climate)**.

   d)   Atmospheric pressure is measured in **(kilograms / millibars)**.

   e)   Air pressure is shown on a synoptic chart with **(isobars / isograms)**.

   f)   In a hurricane, air pressure is **(low / high)**.

Q2   A weather station symbol is shown below. From the list, choose
the correct words to describe the weather shown by the symbol.

clear sky	complete cloud cover	light breeze
strong gale	north-easterly wind	drizzle
hail	south-westerly wind	

Q3   Draw a weather station symbol to show three-eighths cloud cover,
force 4 wind from the north-east and snow showers.

Q4   Name the fronts that the symbols below represent.

   a)   ●●●●●

   b)   ▲▲▲▲▲

   c)   ●▲●▲

Q5   The lines showing air pressure on a map are usually a roughly circular shape.
How can you tell the difference between a high and a low pressure system?

Q6   Copy and complete the chart of selected wind speeds below by filling in the gaps:

Speed in knots	Symbol	Description	Beaufort number
8-12		light breeze	
28-32	⟍⟍○		
	▲○		10

Weather station information can be added to satellite images to make synoptic charts more accurate.

Q1 What are the main weather aspects that can be seen on the following images?

    a) visible images

    b) infra-red images

Q2 On an infra-red image, what do the light colours tell us about the weather?

Q3 Satellite images help show where fronts and isobars should be drawn for a low pressure system. Look at the satellite image below and answer the questions.

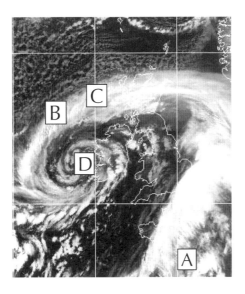

    a) Which letter shows the centre of the low pressure system?

    b) Which two letters would part of a weather front be drawn between on a synoptic chart of the low pressure system?

        i) A and D

        ii) B and C

        iii) C and D

    c) Which letter shows where the highest air pressure is most likely to be?

Q4 Which one of the following best describes where warm and cold fronts are found?

    a) Along the middle of a line of cloud.

    b) Across the darkest areas of the satellite image.

    c) Along the edges of the cloud formations.

    d) In areas with small flecks of cloud.

Weather Hazards — Hurricanes

Q1   Read the travel feature below and then answer the questions about it.

TRAVEL FEATURE — HOLIDAY HURRICANE RISK

The risk of hurricanes in the Caribbean is small, but worse in late summer and early autumn. A safe way to have a Caribbean holiday at this time is to go on a cruise. Weather forecasts may warn of a 'weather bully', but a cruise ship can avoid an area with hurricane warnings. With a land-based holiday, on the other hand, you would just have to suffer.

Florida is popular for holidays but people often forget the risk of hurricanes. Even having a hurricane pass some distance away can bring wet and windy weather for several days. The occasional hurricane usually moves in from the east — over the warm tropical sea — and then turns northwards inland. The wind speed can reduce inland but may still be worse than the strongest winds in the UK. Such weather conditions can easily ruin a holiday.

---

  a)   Why might people go to tropical areas for holidays if there is a risk of hurricanes?

  b)   How does weather forecasting make travelling by ship safer?

  c)   What problems are likely to be experienced if a hurricane does occur on holiday?

  d)   What happens to the wind speed when the hurricane moves inland?

  e)   Describe how a hurricane might form over the sea near the Caribbean and Florida.

Q2   Copy and complete the sentences below by choosing
the correct word or phrase from each pair.

  a)   Hurricanes start within **(5 to 30 / 8 to 15)** degrees of the Equator.

  b)   The temperature has to be higher than **(26°C / 20°C)**.

  c)   Hurricanes probably get their energy from **(water evaporating rapidly / lightning)**.

  d)   A hurricane's life-span is about **(3 to 5 / 7 to 14)** days.

  e)   The calm eye of a hurricane is **(30 to 50 km across / usually under 50 m across)**.

  f)   Wind speeds average **(120 / 160)** km per hour.

  g)   Very heavy rain comes from large **(cumulonimbus / cumulus)** clouds.

Q3   Several recent films have been made about tornadoes.

  a)   Describe the main differences between a hurricane and a tornado.

  b)   Why do you think tornadoes might be a popular theme in films?

Q1   Answer the questions below about drought.

     a)   What is drought?

     b)   Explain how drought can lead to famine.

     c)   Name a country affected by extreme drought in the past.

Q2   Match the beginnings of the sentences below with their correct endings.

After a drought, agricultural land...	...those who are weaker are worst affected.
Reservoirs dry up in a drought, so...	...there may be effects on the country's workforce.
Many children die in a famine because...	...can take a long time to recover.
Many people migrate away, so...	...there may be water shortages for many years.

Q3   Copy and complete the sentences below by choosing the correct word from each pair.

     a)   Relief aid is a **(short / long)** -term response to drought.

     b)   Growing crops which can better cope with drought
        is a **(short / long)** -term response to drought.

     c)   Better transport links would **(increase / decrease)**
        the speed of relief efforts.

     d)   As a long-term response to drought, the population could
        be taught how to **(reduce / increase)** water consumption.

Q4   Which of the following factors might make the consequences of drought worse in LEDCs?

high levels of tourism	reliance on local food and water
poor communications	extent of coastal erosion
poor transport links	lack of money
high chance of flooding	limited medical supplies

World Biomes

Q1   On the map of Africa and Europe below, seven of the main biomes are shown and labelled 1 to 7. For each number, write the correct names of each biome from the list.

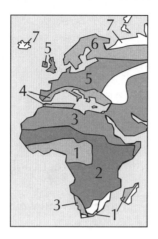

Temperate deciduous forest

Savanna (tropical) grasslands

Tundra

Desert

Tropical forest

Mediterranean

Coniferous forest

Q2   In which of the areas below are tropical grasslands found?

Amazon basin   **Greenland**

Russia   **Central Africa**

Q3   Describe the plant communities found in:

a)   tropical rainforests

b)   savanna grasslands

Q4   The words relating to biomes below are spelt incorrectly.
For each, write out the correct spelling and give a brief definition.

a)   echosystem   b)   equatoriel

c)   fire-resistent   d)   canapy lair

Q5   What is the word used for a plant community where human activity
has arrested succession and altered the natural vegetation?

Q6   Describe five ways in which coniferous trees are
adapted to survive in cold northern areas.

Soils and their Processes

Q1 Read the following paragraph. For each letter, (a) to (g), choose
the best term from those below to describe each phrase:

A worm's eye view of soil

Lower down **the rock breaks up (a)**, producing minerals. On top are **leaves (b)**
that worms drag down and eat. This decomposition makes **fertile soil (c)**. Rain soaks
down and **washes these plant foods to lower levels (d)**.

Woodlice and other small creatures (e) break up rotting branches. Worms avoid
the **waterlogged blue-grey sections of soil (f)**. These contain **liquids that make life
uncomfortable for worms (g)** — they prefer the soil below grass.

Organisms	Acid, pH 5 or lower	Humus	Leaching
Organic matter	Gleyed layer of podsol	Weathering	

Q2 Are the following sentences true or false?

a) Podsolisation occurs under coniferous forest when snow melt
leaches (washes down) minerals, creating acid humus.

b) In a hot desert, water tends to move upwards through the soil,
depositing salt on the surface when it evaporates.

c) Leeches digest the roots of trees, making humus.

d) Gleying occurs after farmers drain water out of soil.

e) In tropical soils, the upper soil layers tend to be red or yellow.

Q3 Join each word to its correct ending.

Texture	...is black when there is a lot of organic matter.
Structure	...is measured in pH — usually 5 (acid) to 8 (alkaline).
Colour	...can be sandy, clay, silt, etc.
Acidity	...can be of crumbly or blocky particles.

Q4 Look at the soil profiles below.
For each soil, name both the soil type and the biome where it is found.

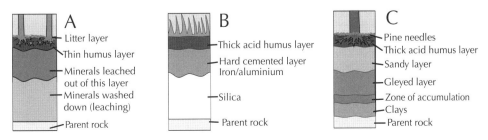

A
- Litter layer
- Thin humus layer
- Minerals leached out of this layer
- Minerals washed down (leaching)
- Parent rock

B
- Thick acid humus layer
- Hard cemented layer Iron/aluminium
- Silica
- Parent rock

C
- Pine needles
- Thick acid humus layer
- Sandy layer
- Gleyed layer
- Zone of accumulation
- Clays
- Parent rock

Savanna Grassland Conservation

Q1   Write the correct definitions for each of these uses of savanna grassland areas.

Arable means

a)   farming by Arabs.

b)   growing crops like millet and maize.

c)   keeping horses in stables.

Cash cropping means

a)   using large areas to grow crops like tobacco and cotton.

b)   laundering money.

c)   buying crops from abroad.

Q2   List three other uses of savanna grasslands not mentioned in Q1.

Q3   Copy out this paragraph about land use conflicts, filling in the gaps with the correct words.

_____ go on safaris to see wildlife such as elephants.

Conservationists work to stop _____ killing animals for ivory and fur.

Cash crop farmers force small scale farmers to use _____ farming land.

Desertification is caused by _____ farming, and makes the land useless.

Q4   Look at the diagram below. Describe how two of the things labelled on the diagram cause the other two.

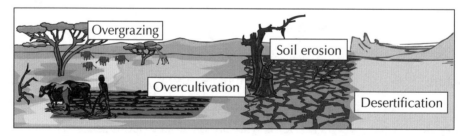

Overgrazing

Soil erosion

Overcultivation

Desertification

Q5   A desert can be a disaster when it spreads. Match up the words from the first column to their correct endings from the second column, to make five different methods of preventing desertification.

Terracing the slopes...	...that are good for building materials.
Planting hedges...	...made from cow manure.
Using land less intensively...	...to stop soil erosion by wind.
Planting trees...	...to reduce soil run-off.
Using fertiliser...	...by letting it lie fallow sometimes.

Deforestation and Conservation

Q1 The diagram below shows five reasons why deforestation is happening in Brazil.
List the five reasons and explain them.

Q2 There are arguments both for and against deforestation. Write two lists, one <u>for</u>
deforestation and one <u>against</u>, putting each of the following points into the correct list.

    a) More than half of all medicines were originally discovered in trees and plants in forests.

    b) Many LEDCs' economies rely on exporting timber from forests.

    c) Many native tribes live in forests.

    d) Firewood is essential in many LEDCs.

    e) Removing forests reduces rainfall, causing drought.

    f) Trees absorb carbon dioxide and so help to reduce global warming.

    g) Most of the nutrients in a tropical rainforest are in the trees and not in the soil.

    h) Wildlife habitats should be preserved to maintain biodiversity.

    i) MEDCs such as the UK deforested large areas when they were developing.

Q3 Malaysia has a good conservation policy. Which two of the following does the
Malaysian government insist on in order to control felling of hardwood trees?

    a) Replanting a tree for each one felled.

    b) Shooting tree poachers.

    c) Using hand saws instead of chain saws.

    d) Only felling mature trees of a certain age and height.

Q4 Give two reasons why some people say that MEDCs are equally responsible
for deforestation in LEDCs as the LEDCs themselves are.

Sustainable Development in Forests

Q1 How many hectares of the world's forests disappear every year?

   a) 1200

   b) 12 000

   c) 12 000 000

   d) 12 000 000 000

Q2 Why are many people reluctant to change the ways they use forests?

Q3 Copy out these sentences about sustainable forestry techniques,
selecting the correct words to fill the spaces.

   The most common type of forestry is _____, which involves cutting
   down vast amounts of trees. An alternative to this is _____, where
   trees are air-lifted out by helicopter — this is also known as _____.
   Replanting is another method of preserving forests. Trees are _____
   by trees of the right type for the area — recently, _____ have been
   introduced to make sure _____ companies do this.
   Another sustainable forestry technique is _____, when areas of forest
   are set aside for particular uses.

Q4 Write three sentences by matching up each type of
sustainable forestry to the reason why it is useful.

   Selective logging...   ...allows the forest to recover naturally.

   Horse logging...   ...can maintain a strong gene pool.

   Natural regeneration...   ...reduces the need for trucks.

Q5 Describe two ways of promoting the sustainable use of forests,
and give an example of each.

Q6 List two ways of discouraging bad practice in forestry.

Q7 Explain how debt-for-nature swaps can reduce the need for large scale deforestation.

Population Distribution

Q1 The map shows the distribution of the world's population:

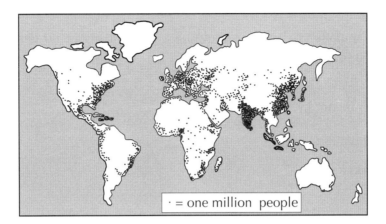

· = one million people

Copy out the following passage. Include the correct words from the pairs.
Give the name of an appropriate country in the spaces.

The population distribution of the world is very **(even / uneven)**. Places with lots of
people include **(wealthy / poor)** industrialised countries, such as _____ ,
_____ and eastern USA and **(wealthy / poor)** countries with
(slowly / rapidly) growing populations such as _____ and
_____ . Places with few people are usually **(habitable / hostile)**
environments such as _____ .

Q2 Briefly describe why the following are good places to live:

a) river valleys

b) lowland plains

c) areas rich in natural resources

d) coastal plains

Q3 Decide whether each of the following statements is true or false.
Rewrite each false statement so that it is correct.

a) Areas with extreme climates are usually highly populated.

b) Arid areas with a lack of precipitation are sparsely populated.

c) Areas of high altitude have fertile soils and gentle slopes,
so farming is easy and lots of people live in mountainous areas.

Population Density

Q1   Give a definition of population density. Include the unit of measurement in your answer.

Q2   Explain why population density is not always a useful measure for describing the distribution of population.

Q3   Explain what is meant by the following terms:

    a)   overpopulation

    b)   underpopulation

    c)   optimum population

Q4   Copy out the table below. Fill in the table to show whether the population density in the named places is HIGH or LOW.

Country	Number of people per km^2 (1996 figures)	High or low density
United Kingdom	238	
Brazil	18.5	
Japan	333	
Netherlands	374	
Australia	2.4	

Q5   Study the OS map extract below. The map is of an area north of Keswick in the Lake District. Give <u>two</u> reasons why there are no settlements on the extract. Refer to features you can see on the map in your answer.

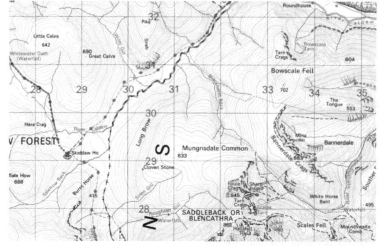

© Crown copyright, License no. 100034841

Q1 Copy out the sentences matching the following terms to their correct definition:

natural decrease　　**birth rate**　　**migration**　　**death rate**　　**natural increase**

a) The _____ is the number of live babies born per thousand of the population per year.

b) The _____ is the number of deaths per thousand of the population per year.

c) _____ describes people moving into or out of a country.

d) If the birth rate is higher than the death rate, the difference between them is called the _____ .

e) If the death rate is higher than the birth rate, the difference between them is called the _____ .

Q2 Name the two main types of migration, and explain the difference between them.

Q3 Copy the diagram of the demographic transition model.
Fill in the spaces with the most appropriate words.

Stage 1 High fluctuating	Stage 2 Early _____	Stage 3 ____ _____	Stage 4 ____ fluctuating	Stage 5 _____
Birth Rate Total Population Death Rate				
High birth & death rates cancel each other out	_____ falls _____ remains high	Death rate _____ Birth rate _____	_____ birth & death rates cancel each other out	Birth rate falls below _____
Population remains stable and low	Population begins to _____	Population still _____	Population high but _____	Population _____
e.g. Rainforest tribes	e.g. _____	e.g. China	e.g. _____	e.g. _____

Population Structure

Q1 Study the population pyramids below. Match each shape to the place it is most typical of. Put your answers in a copy of the table.

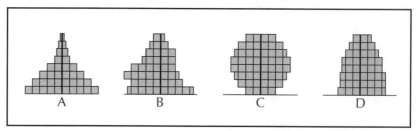

Description of Pyramid	Pyramid letter
An MEDC	
An LEDC	
A fast-growing capital city in an LEDC	
An MEDC with a declining population	

Q2 Study the population pyramid below and then answer the questions below.

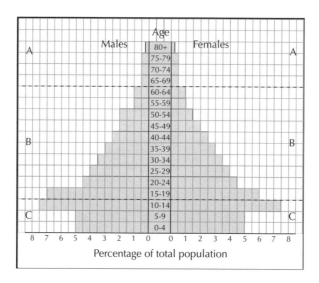

Percentage of total population

a) What percentage of the population are males between the ages of 15–19?

b) What percentage of the population are females between the ages of 50–54?

c) What percentage of the population is between 60–64 years old?

d) What percentage of the population is between 0–9 years old?

e) Which part of the pyramid (A, B or C) represents the economically active population?

f) Which part of the pyramid (A, B or C) represents the young dependant population?

g) Which part of the pyramid (A, B or C) represents the elderly dependant population?

Q1   Give a definition of the term 'dependency ratio'.

Q2   Use a calculator to calculate the dependency ratio for the USA and
Uganda (to 1 decimal place). Use the figures in the table below:

Country	USA	Uganda
Young dependants	60 300	12 000
Old dependants	35 000	500
Economically active	187 000	11 000

Q3   Copy out and complete these sentences, using the correct words from the pairs.

a)   Countries with a **(high / low)** dependency ratio of over 100 are **(LEDCs / MEDCs)**.

b)   Countries with a dependency ratio of between
50 and 70 are usually **(LEDCs / MEDCs)**.

c)   **(High / Low)** numbers of children are common in LEDCs.

d)   High numbers of **(elderly people / children)** are common in MEDCs.

Q4   Outline the different problems that the two countries below
will have in trying to support their dependent populations.
Give <u>at least three</u> separate problems for each country.

a)   Problems in Uganda

b)   Problems in the USA

Migration

Q1 Using the phrases below, write out three sentences about migration, by matching the correct ending to each beginning:

International migration is when...   ...people move a short distance within the same region.

Regional migration is when...   ...people move from one country to another.

Local migration is when...   ...people move between regions within the same country.

Q2 Describe what is meant by 'push' and 'pull' factors.
Give three examples of each.

Q3 The table below shows terms and descriptions for the movement of people.
Copy and complete the table.

Term			Immigrant
Definition	Someone moving out of a country.	Someone moving from one place to another.	

Q4 Give a definition of the following terms:

a) Refugee

b) Rural-urban migration

c) Counter-urbanisation

d) Brain drain

Q1 Copy the diagram. Complete the cycle using the appropriate phrase from the ones given. The first one has been done for you.

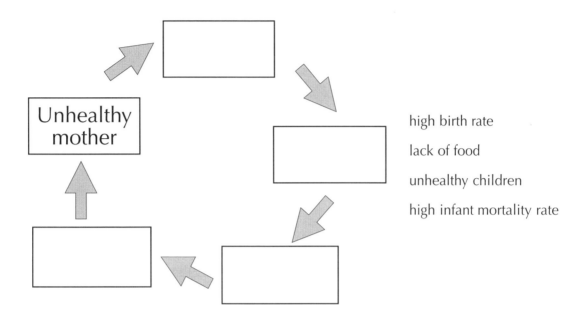

Unhealthy
mother

high birth rate

lack of food

unhealthy children

high infant mortality rate

Q2 LEDCs want to break this vicious circle and reduce the birth rate.

a) Describe two ways of slowing the birth rate.

b) Suggest two reasons why these solutions can be difficult to introduce.

Q3 Increasing the food supply is one way of tackling the problem of malnutrition and famine in LEDCs. However, there can be some negative consequences. State <u>three different</u> ways in which food supply can be increased. For each method explain one problem it may cause.

Q4 Governments can either encourage or refuse immigration into their country. Copy out this paragraph about immigration, filling in the blanks with the correct words.

Governments sometimes give _____ to companies to persuade them

to locate in _____ areas.

This improves the area's economy, because people move there for _____.

Settlement Site and Situation

Q1 **Make correct sentences from the following phrases:**

A settlement's site is...   ...high points or in meanders.

Wet point sites are found...   ...its location relative to other places.

Dry point sites are on...   ...near rivers or springs.

Defensive sites originated on...   ...higher ground avoiding floods.

A settlement's situation is...   ...the land it is built on.

Q2 **In the past settlements were often built near places with a good natural supply of wood or stone. Why was this important?**

Q3 **From the list below copy out the factors that would have been important to people who were choosing <u>defensive sites</u> in the past.**

bridging points

direction of wind

height

winter temperatures

presence of natural barriers

Q4 **Use this diagram to answer the questions:**

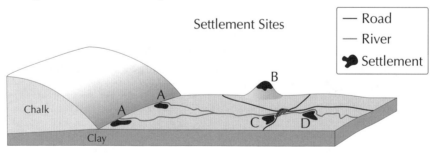

Settlement Sites

— Road
— River
🐾 Settlement

a)   Which site factor led to the choice of the sites marked A?

b)   Give <u>two</u> advantages of the height of site B.

c)   Give <u>two</u> reasons for the choice of site C.

d)   What kind of site is site D known as?

e)   Which site is the best example of a dry point site?

Q1 **Look at the hierarchy pyramid.**
Copy and complete the table using the letters on the pyramid.

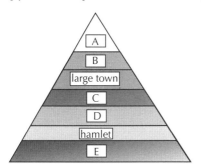

Settlement	Letter
small town	
city	
village	
conurbation	
isolated dwelling	

Q2 **Answer the following questions:**

a)   As the settlement size increases what happens to the number of settlements of each size?

b)   What usually happens to the populations and numbers of services with progression up the hierarchy of settlements?

Q3 **List the five of these terms which have the same meaning:**

sphere of influence	hinterland	sports field
market place	catchment area	urban field
circle of affluence	area land market area	suggestion zone

Q4 **The scattergraph below shows settlements in Shropshire.**

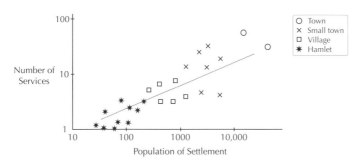

Scattergraph of population and number of services in Shropshire

a)   What general relationship does the graph above illustrate?

b)   Copy out the <u>three</u> services from the list that are likely to be found in a small village.

post office   jewellery shop   newsagent   infant school   university

c)   Why do villages not have the other two in the list above?

d)   Are the services you chose in b) low or high order services?

The Function of Settlements

Q1 What kind of things can geographers look at to find out what the main function of a settlement is?

Q2 Describe these common settlement functions.

    a) Administrative centre.

    b) Retail function.

Q3 Copy out the statements below and use the words and phrases from the list below to complete them.

    ports   **resorts**   **industrial centres**   **cultural centres**

    a)   Settlements with a reputation for history and education are known as

        _____.

    b)   _____ such as Skegness are holiday centres, often on the coast.

    c)   _____ are settlements that have developed around the import and export of goods.

    d)   Settlements where manufacturing is the main employer are known

        as _____.

Q4 Write down whether each of the statements below is an example of an industrial change, a change in planning policy or a social change.

    a)   The decline of a particular industry (e.g. shipbuilding in Barrow-in-Furness).

    b)   The redevelopment of docklands in London and Salford to reflect local environmental agendas.

    c)   The decline of town centre shopping as out of town retail parks increase.

    d)   Fewer people take traditional seaside holidays in British resorts.

    e)   The availability of grants to encourage the redevelopment of old industrial sites into leisure facilities.

    f)   Property in rural settlements is becoming increasingly sought after by people looking for holiday homes.

Q1   Copy and complete the table to show the land uses on the zones of the Burgess model.
The first one has been done for you.

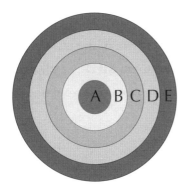

Land use	Letter
medium-quality residential	D
central business district	
high-quality residential	
wholesale light manufacturing	
low-quality residential	

Q2   Answer the following questions about land use in LEDC cities.

a)   Where in the city are shanty towns usually found?

b)   What types of building are most likely to be situated along the
main roads into the cities?

c)   Name <u>two</u> problems that face the people who live on the edge
of cities and work in the CBD in LEDCs.

Q3   Complete the following sentences a)-f) by using the correct endings from i)-vi).

a)   The Central Business District (CBD)...

b)   Dormitory villages on the edge of cities...

c)   Housing near the CBD...

d)   'Gentrification' describes the process where...

e)   The cost of land and property in the CBD is...

f)   Wholesale manufacturing is mostly associated with the...

i)   ...house people who like to work in the city and live in the country.

ii)   ...land and property in the inner city is developed and turned into desirable housing.

iii)   ...tends to be old terraces.

iv)   ...expensive due to the intense competition for space.

v)   ...is the commercial centre of the city.

vi)   ...zone of transition or inner city.

Urbanisation

Q1   Copy the following passage including the correct words from the pair in brackets:

Urbanisation takes place when an **(increasing / decreasing)** proportion of the world's population are living in urban areas. Urbanisation only occurs when the **(growth rate / birth rate)** of **(cities / villages)** is greater than the growth rate of the whole population. Urbanisation is happening **(only in MEDCs / all over the world)**. Urbanisation has created lots of **(millionaire / billionaire)** cities.

Q2   Write a sentence for each of the following, describing why they have caused urbanisation.

a)   The industrial revolution

b)   Redevelopment schemes

c)   Increased housing in cities

d)   People searching for employment in LEDCs

Q3   Define the term 'millionaire city' and give <u>two</u> examples.

Q4   Urbanisation can cause problems in both the countryside and in cities.
Make a copy of the table and fill it in using the list of problems on the right.

Problems for the countryside	Problems for the city

overcrowding

ageing population

fewer extended families

shortage of housing

high birth rate

reliance on agriculture

little inward investment

strained infrastructure

economic stagnation

shanty towns

Q1 Choose the <u>three</u> most appropriate words and phrases from the list below to describe the problems associated with transport in many MEDC cities. Explain your choices.

congestion

public transport unable to meet demand

squatter settlements

pollution

market gardening

Q2 Give <u>two</u> reasons why many companies have abandoned inner city sites for manufacturing.

Q3 Is the following statement true or false?

'**Employment in inner cities has vastly increased in the last twenty years.**'

Q4 Governments in MEDCs have introduced policies with the aim of reducing inner city problems. Explain what the following government schemes involve:

a) Urban renewal schemes

b) Gentrification

Q5 Look at the diagram below and answer the questions.

a) What effect does the diagram illustrate?

b) Give one common cause of this effect.

c) Explain how this leads to the effect shown in the diagram.

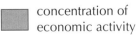

movement of economic activity outwards

concentration of economic activity

Q6 Define the term 'conurbation' and give an example from the UK.

Urban Problems in LEDCs

Q1   Explain why shanty towns grow on the fringes of LEDC cities.

Q2   Below is a list of factors that are linked to the problem of overcrowding in LEDC cities. Copy out these factors, placing each one under a heading of either 'LAND' (if the problem is one of competition for land) or 'SERVICES' (if the problem is one of pressure on services).

a)   Poor sanitation

b)   Shanty towns built on dangerous ground

c)   Demand for health care

d)   Lack of clean water

e)   Demand for houses near to places of work

f)   No efficient waste disposal

Q3   Explain why rural-urban migration makes problems in LEDC cities worse.

Q4   Are the following statements about LEDC cities true or false?

a)   Sewerage systems generally cope well with the city waste.

b)   Water supplies and crops are often contaminated with sewage.

c)   Shanty towns are often built on dangerous rubbish tips.

d)   Travelling across LEDC cities is usually quick and easy.

Q5   Describe an example of how LEDCs have tried to solve the following problems:

a)   Housing shortage and the formation of shanty towns.

b)   Unemployment.

Q1   Answer the following questions:

   a)   What does the term 'rural-urban fringe' mean?

   b)   Name <u>three</u> leisure activities that are common in rural-urban fringes.

Q2   Describe why 'new towns' were needed. Give an example from the UK.

Q3   Answer the following questions:

   a) What are greenbelts?

   b) When were they introduced?

   c) Why have some greenbelts been released for development?

Q4   Give an example of a planning scheme designed to cope with
increased demand for housing in an MEDC city.

Q5   Copy out one of the statements below that you think
describes the best method of checking urban sprawl.

   a)   Stop people from moving to the countryside.

   b)   Make sure that urban growth is carefully planned.

   c)   Build more tower blocks for people to live in.

   d)   Stop building roads.

The Farm as a System

Q1   Is farming classified as a primary, secondary or tertiary industry?

Q2   Copy the table of economic and physical inputs to the farm system.
Copy the inputs on the right into the correct column:

Economic inputs	Physical inputs

climate

capital

pesticides

weather

young stock

labour

EU subsidies

buildings and machinery

soil

fertiliser

transport

seeds

relief

Q3   Name <u>two</u> things which make up feedback in the farm system.

Q4   The farmer is important in the system because he / she is a 'decision maker'.
Suggest <u>three</u> things that farmers have to make decisions about when running their farms.

Q5   The prices of produce are very important to farmers.
Explain what happens to the prices farmers get for their produce in these situations:

     a)   There is a very good harvest.

     b)   There is a very poor harvest.

Q6   Name <u>two</u> hazards which can affect how much profit a farmer makes.

Q1 Match up each phrase a) - c) with its correct definition i) - iii).

a) Arable farms   i) produce both animals and crops

b) Mixed farms   ii) specialise in rearing animals

c) Pastoral farms   iii) specialise in growing crops

Q2 Copy and complete the table, giving a definition for each term.

Term	Definition
Intensive farming	
Extensive farming	
Subsistence farming	
Commercial farming	

Q3 Give brief answers to the following questions:

a) What is plantation agriculture?

b) What is factory farming?

c) What is shifting cultivation?

Q4 Classify these examples of farming. The first one has been done for you as an example. Use three terms (like those in the example) for each one.

a) A dairy farm of 140 hectares, Somerset. = Pastoral, intensive and commercial.

b) A British battery chicken farm.

c) A poor family's two hectare vegetable plot in Nepal.

d) Wheat growing on the Canadian Prairies.

Distribution of Farming Types

Q1 Make a sketch of or trace the map of the UK below.
Add labels from the list underneath to show the distribution of farming types in the UK.

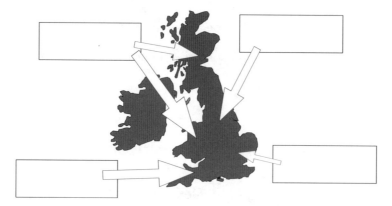

Extensive sheep farming

mixed farming on large-scale commercial farms

intensive cereal farming

intensive dairy farming

Q2 Copy the table below. Put the examples of farming from the list on the right into the right box to show what kind of climate they take place in.

	Examples
Temperate	
Tropical	
Extreme	

Tuareg herding in sub-Saharan Africa

Horticulture in NW Europe

Inuits in North Canada

Coffee plantations in Brazil

Sheep farming in New Zealand

Banana plantations in Costa Rica

Q3 Provide brief answers to these questions:

a) Explain why upland areas of the UK are unsuited to arable farming.

b) Explain why lowland areas in the South West of England produce good pastures.

c) Explain why East Anglia suits 'agribusiness'.

Q4 Write down whether each of these is a political, market, labour or physical factor which affects farming.

a) Type of soil

b) High demand for dairy products

c) Ageing population

d) Government grants

Farming in the European Union (EU)

Q1   What does 'CAP' stand for?

Q2   Read through this article about CAP written by a farmer
and then answer the questions below.

> "Food shortages during the Second World War alarmed politicians because
> they realised just how easily European countries could end up without
> enough food. The CAP was an attempt to encourage farmers to produce
> more food by giving us subsidies. CAP worked by guaranteeing farmers
> a standard price for produce regardless of prices outside Europe.
> You could say that farmers were protected by CAP from having to
> compete with cheap imports from outside the EU.
> We increased our yields by using more fertilisers and pesticides
> and by ploughing woodlands and hedgerows.
> Of course, the down side of all this is that we actually ended up
> producing far too much food, and huge 'food mountains' of butter, milk,
> wine and grain were created. After a period of storage, much of this surplus
> produce was destroyed. I find this really annoying because there are lots
> of people who are starving in other parts of the world."

a)   Why was CAP introduced?

b)   What was the aim of CAP?

c)   Why would cheap imports be a threat to EU farmers?

d)   How did CAP protect farmers from this threat?

e)   Use the information in the passage to write a paragraph
to explain <u>three</u> major problems that were caused by CAP.

Q3   **Since 1945 miles of hedgerows have been removed in
Britain to make farming more efficient.**

a)   Give <u>three</u> reasons why hedgerows have been removed.

b)   Give <u>three</u> reasons why hedgerows are important to the environment.

Farming in the European Union (EU)

Q1   The EU introduced milk quotas in 1984 in an attempt to control milk production.

    a)   Explain how the quota system works.

    b)   Explain <u>two</u> problems with the milk quota system.

Q2   This question is about set-aside. Copy out the following statements and add the correct missing word or words from the box. Use each word only once.

    a)   Under set-aside policy, farmers receive _____ from the EU.

    b)   Set-aside requires farmers to leave land _____.

    c)   The aim of set-aside is to reduce _____.

    d)   Set-aside began in 1988 and was _____.

    e)   By 1992, cereal farmers were still producing a _____.

    f)   If they wish to benefit from the scheme, farmers with over 20 _____ of land must now leave _____ of it as set-aside.

    g)   Set-aside land should be left for at least _____, but can be used for other purposes such as _____ and _____, or left _____.

surplus	voluntary	hectares	15%
wildlife areas	uncultivated	woodland	
production	five years	subsidies	fallow

Q3   Answer the following questions:

    a)   Explain what diversification is.

    b)   Give <u>four</u> examples of diversification of farmland.

Q4   Answer the following questions:

    a)   What does ESA stand for?

    b)   What is the aim of ESAs?

    c)   Give <u>two</u> examples of ESAs from the UK.

Q1 Copy the flow chart which is about some of the problems associated with subsistence farming in LEDCs. Fill it in using the phrases below. The first one has been done for you.

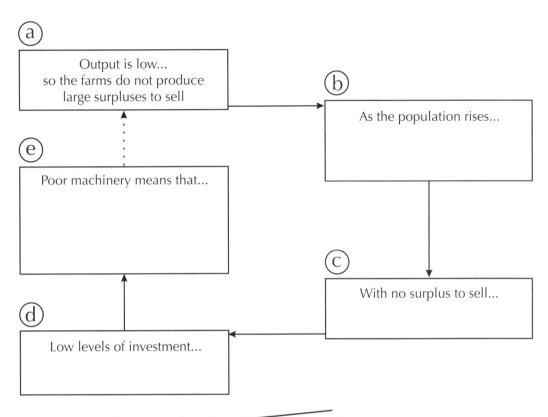

(a) Output is low... so the farms do not produce large surpluses to sell

(b) As the population rises...

(e) Poor machinery means that...

(c) With no surplus to sell...

(d) Low levels of investment...

...so the farms do not produce large surpluses to sell.

...farmers have no money to invest.

...mean that the machinery is poor quality.

...it is more difficult to feed everyone.

...yields remain low.

Q2 Explain why the flow chart you have drawn in Q1 could be labelled a 'poverty trap'.

Q3 List and explain <u>three</u> advantages and <u>three</u> disadvantages of plantations in LEDCs.

The Green Revolution

Q1   Explain what the term 'high yield variety' means when used in relation to food production.

Q2   Explain why each of the following help to increase yields.

    a)   Planting dwarf varieties

    b)   Growing plants with smaller root systems

    c)   Growing plants with an ability to withstand common diseases

    d)   Using plants with shorter growing seasons

Q3   Make two lists from the sentences below.
One should be a list of successes of the Green Revolution and one of the failures.

    i)   Rice production has doubled.

    ii)   Some farms are very small and farmers can't afford the new seeds and fertiliser.

    iii)   New farming methods have created new jobs, e.g. drivers and mechanics.

    iv)   Many farm workers migrate to the cities, adding to the urban problems.

    v)   There are new jobs in factories making chemicals.

    vi)   People have surplus food to sell and therefore have more money.

    vii)   The use of machinery has caused farm workers to lose their jobs.

    viii)   Poorer farmers are afraid to change to new methods.

    ix)   Schemes for borrowing money are not well developed.

    x)   Two crops per year are possible with irrigation.

Q4   What is 'appropriate technology'? Why is it considered important?

Q5   Copy out the following statements about the Green Revolution
and write T next to them if they are true and F if they are false.

    a)   The Green Revolution is the name for changes in farming practices
in LEDCs, intended to increase yields.

    b)   It began in the 1920s.

    c)   It was introduced because of the need to increase the output of cash crops.

    d)   It was introduced because of a need to increase outputs of subsistence crops.

Farming and Soil Erosion

Q1 Write five sentences to explain the causes of soil erosion based on the following factors:

a) Ploughing

b) Deforestation

c) Monocultures and fertilisers

d) Overgrazing

e) Removal of hedgerows

Q2 Give a brief explanation of each of the methods labelled a - f, which are designed to reduce soil erosion.

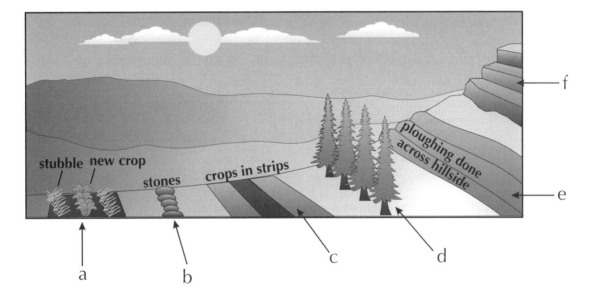

Q3 Which of these statements about desertification is true?
Copy out the right sentence.

Desertification happens mostly in MEDCs.

Desertification is the result of unsustainable farming.

Desertification is where nomadic people leave land to recover after they have cultivated it.

Q4 'Desertification cannot be reversed.'
Do you agree or disagree with this statement? Explain your answer.

More Environmental Questions

Q1   Decide whether each of the following statements about irrigation is true or false.
Rewrite each false statement so that it is correct.

    a)   Irrigation is used in both LEDCs and MEDCs when the water supply is inadequate.

    b)   Irrigation schemes are all large-scale projects such as the Aswan High Dam in Egypt.

    c)   Most large-scale schemes are single purpose.

    d)   Irrigation can increase yields.

Q2   Copy and complete this table to show how these problems of irrigation are caused.

Problem	Cause
Reduced river flow	
Salinisation	
Increased aridity	

Q3   Describe the consequences for the environment of:

    a)   Habitat destruction

    b)   Overuse of fertilisers

    c)   Use of pesticides

Q4   Copy out the statement which gives the correct definition of organic farming.

Organic farming only applies to crops — meat can't be farmed organically.

Organic farming is farming without the use of chemical fertilisers and pesticides.

Organic farmers only grow crops which are native to the area they are cultivating.

Q5   What is the aim of sustainable farming? Give <u>two</u> examples.

Classification of Industry

Q1 The grid below describes the four types of industry. Copy it and fill in the blanks.

Type of industry	What it involves	Example 1	Example 2
Primary			
	Manufacturing a product	House building	
Tertiary		Advertising	
	Research and development		Crop research

Q2 All the companies below were involved in making a book and getting it to the bookshop.

The New Zealand Forestry Company

The PaperMakery
Finest quality paper

Harvey & Daughter
Manufacturers of books since 1950

TZC Laboratories
Tree & plant genetics

Baffin & Braithwaite
BOOKSHOP

Kutter & Company
Logger

a) Which two companies are primary industries?

b) The finished product of one of the manufacturers is the starting point for another manufacturer. Is this product logs, wood pulp, paper or books?

c) Which company provides a tertiary service directly to the public?

d) Write down the steps involved in converting tree seedlings into the books we buy.

e) Is this statement true or false? 'TZC laboratories are a secondary manufacturer'.

Q3 Fill in the blanks using any of the words 'primary', 'secondary', tertiary', or 'quaternary'.

A cook who makes the meals served in a North Sea oil rig has a

_____ job working in a _____ industry.

Industry as a System

Q1 The diagram below shows industry as a **system**.
Copy the diagram and answer the questions.

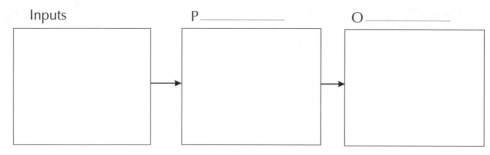

Inputs   P_____   O_____

a) Label the other two boxes to the right of 'inputs'.

b) Draw an arrow to show feedback in this system.

c) Put the words below in the correct box to show a
   system diagram of a factory making chocolates.

remove chocolates from the moulds	capital	top quality boxes of chocolates
mix the ingredients profit	foil for wrappings	sugar cocoa beans
wrap the chocolates in foil	pour liquid into moulds	cleaning factory machinery

Q2 Read this newspaper clipping from the *Newtown Echo* and answer the questions.

> Newtown is reeling. The Komfort furniture factory, Newtown's main employer,
> is to close with the loss of 550 jobs.
>
> The road haulage distribution centre that delivers Komfort furniture to retailers
> across the UK will also close. Job losses are likely for local manufacturers of
> stain-proof fabrics, springs, castors, a dyeing plant and a foam-cutting business.
> However, the BXE Furniture chainstore may take advantage of the increase
> in the number of skilled workers available by expanding its new factory at
> the Newtown Interchange Industrial Estate.

a) Name two types of component that Komfort use in making furniture.

b) What is the correct name for the way one industry relies on others?

c) Why is the furniture factory closing bad news for Newtown's lorry drivers?

d) Why do you think that BXE Furniture built their factory so
   near to another furniture factory?

Q1 **Copy the diagram and fill in the blanks with the four main factors which affect industrial location using the list on the right.**

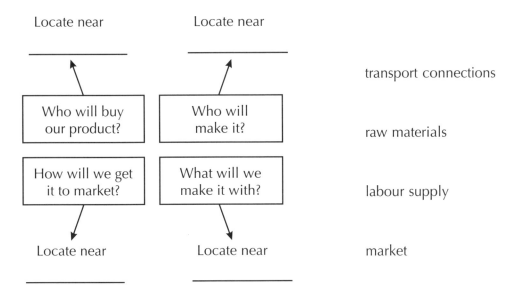

Locate near _____

Locate near _____

Who will buy our product?

Who will make it?

How will we get it to market?

What will we make it with?

Locate near _____

Locate near _____

transport connections

raw materials

labour supply

market

Q2 **Answer the following questions:**

a) Give <u>two</u> reasons why the north of England became particularly heavily industrialised during the industrial revolution.

b) Which raw material was abundant in Wales and the area around Newcastle during the industrial revolution?

c) What type of costs are reduced by locating a factory near raw materials?

Q3 **Answer the following questions:**

a) State <u>two</u> advantages for a company if it locates where there is high unemployment.

b) Why might it be less of an advantage for specialised companies to locate in areas of high unemployment?

c) Why is a place with a large labour supply also a large market?

Q4 **Name a type of industry which needs each of these kinds of labour:**

a) A small, highly skilled workforce.

b) A large number of unskilled staff.

c) An extra group of seasonal staff during the busiest periods.

Location of Industry

Q1   Give three advantages of rail transport and three advantages of road transport
for a business. Think about factors such as cost, accessibility, reliability, etc.

Q2   Suggest whether transport by each of the following
has increased or declined in the last fifty years.

a) rail   b) road   c) air   d) sea

Q3   Copy the diagram and then answer the questions below.

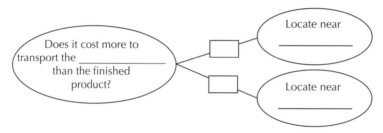

a)   Fill in the blank rectangles with either 'yes' or 'no' in the decision tree above,
and complete the missing words in the ovals.

b)   Give <u>one</u> reason why paper-mills are built near forests.

Q4   Answer the following questions:

a)   What is an 'industrial agglomeration'?

b)   Why are 'assembly industries' often located in industrial agglomerations?

Q5   Describe <u>one</u> government policy which affects industrial location.

Q6   Answer the following questions:

a)   Why is tinned food imported to Britain by sea?

b)   Why are fresh flowers from the Scilly Isles brought to the mainland by helicopter?

c)   Why is a firm making air-conditioning units located near a major road?

d)   Why aren't livestock exported to Europe by air?

Q1   Give two types of problem that increased traffic flow is causing.

Q2   Copy the outline of this diagram, then follow the instructions below.

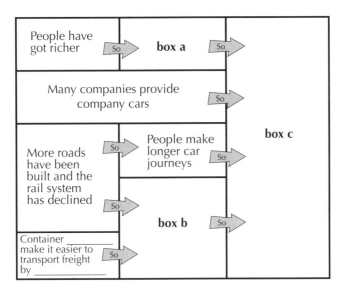

a)   Fill in the blanks in the bottom left box.

b)   Put the phrases below into the correct boxes a-c on the diagram.

'Freight is increasingly carried by road rather than rail.'

'There are more vehicles on the roads.'

'More households can afford two cars.'

Q3   What measures can be taken to solve the problems below?

a)   Everyone tries to travel at rush hour.

b)   Cars go dangerously fast in residential areas.

c)   It is dangerous to cycle in cities.

d)   It's difficult to park in the city centre.

Q4   Answer the following questions:

a)   Explain why building new roads as a solution to congestion sometimes makes the problem worse.

b)   How do new roads damage the environment?

c)   How does congestion affect the economy?

Changing Industry — MEDCs

Q1 **Answer the following questions:**

a)   Give two main reasons why the number of people employed in traditional manufacturing has decreased in Britain in the last fifty years.
Mention raw materials and competition in your answer.

b)   Copy the three sentences below and choose the correct word from the choices.

   i)   Some countries compete with British industry by having **(lower / higher)** wages and **(more / less)** strict pollution controls.

   ii)   Many foreign countries are **(nearer to / further away from)** the remaining sources of raw materials than Britain is.

c)   Why are the last iron and steel works left in South Wales near ports?

d)   Not all the tin in Cornwall has actually been used up
but the last tin mine has closed. Suggest a reason for this.

e)   Give one serious consequence of the decline in manufacture.

Q2 **Which <u>three</u> of the phrases below explain why a lot of industry has moved south in the UK?**

a)   The South is the largest and richest market.

b)   The South has the best transport network.

c)   The South has the highest land and property prices.

d)   The South does not have raw materials such as coal or iron ore.

e)   The South is more convenient for trade with Europe.

Q3 **Which of these pie charts shows the employment structure of the UK in 1945, and which shows its structure in 1995?**

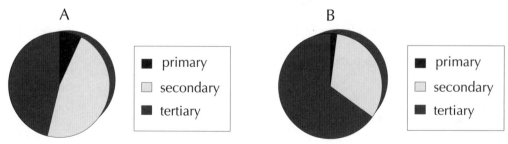

A   B

■ primary   ■ primary
☐ secondary   ☐ secondary
■ tertiary   ■ tertiary

Q4 **Answer the following questions:**

a)   What kind of industries locate in science parks?

b)   Give <u>two</u> factors which attract businesses to science parks.

Changing Industry — LEDCs

Q1   **Answer the following questions:**

a)   Explain the difference between formal and informal industries in LEDCs.

b)   Give <u>two</u> examples of an informal industry.

c)   In which sector — formal or informal — is the level of job security generally highest?

d)   Explain why LEDCs have found it easier to develop their informal sectors than their formal sectors.

Q2   **Answer the following questions:**

a)   What does NIC stand for?

b)   Which of the places below have what are known as 'Tiger Economies'?

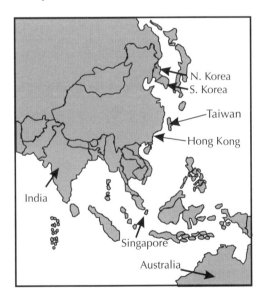

c)   What factors helped the NICs build up their industries?

d)   Which of these products are typical export goods of NICs?

electronic components	**coal**	**wheat**
cars	**coffee beans**	**sports gear**

e)   Are the goods produced in NICs from primary, secondary or tertiary industries?

Multinationals

Q1 **Write down what these abbreviations stand for:**

    a)   MNC

    b)   MEDC

    c)   TNC

    d)   LEDC

    e)   NIC

Q2 **Answer the questions below using the abbreviations in Q1.**

    a)   Do MNCs usually locate their research and development in LEDCs or MEDCs?

    b)   Where do they usually locate their manufacturing?

    c)   Explain why companies might make the above decisions.

Q3 **Why might having low wages and few regulations be an advantage for an LEDC?**

Q4 **Make a table which shows <u>five</u> advantages and <u>five</u> disadvantages of MNCs for the host country.**

Q5 **Are the following statements true or false?**

    a)   'No multinational company can ever be richer than an entire country.'

    b)   'There are no companies from LEDCs which trade in more than one country.'

    c)   'In 1990 the hundred top MNCs controlled around 50% of all world manufacturing.'

Q6 **Give the names of:**

    a)   <u>Four</u> MNCs

    b)   <u>Two</u> types of business that tend to operate on a local scale.

Q1 Answer the following questions:

a) What is recycling'?

b) Give <u>three</u> examples of things that can be recycled.

c) Does recycling lead to an overall increase or decrease in energy use?

Q2 Fill in the blanks in these sentences using the words below.
You won't need to use all the words.

a) There are not always _____ resources to go round.

b) LEDCs produce _____ of the world's resources.

c) MEDCs use _____ of the world's resources.

d) As LEDCs develop they will need an _____ amount of resources.

enough	decreasing	most	all
increasing	many	more	

Q3 Answer the following questions:

a) What is 'stewardship'?

b) Copy and complete these four key things that stewardship involves:

i) R_____ conservation.

ii) Resource s_____.

iii) P_____ control.

iv) Recycling to reduce the amount of w_____ produced.

Energy and Power

Q1 **Copy and complete the following description of energy production using the words supplied below.**

Energy is obtained from _____ like

_____ or _____, which are

converted to _____ at _____.

gas   natural resources   coal   power stations   electricity

Q2 **Copy the table and fill it in so that it shows three renewable sources of energy and three non-renewable sources.**

Renewable	Non-renewable

Q3 **LEDCs like Kenya and Nepal often destroy large areas of forest.**

a) Give <u>two</u> reasons why they need to use so many trees for fuel.

b) Describe <u>two</u> environmental problems that result from this deforestation.

Q4 **What kind of alternative energy sources do the labels a) — d) show?**

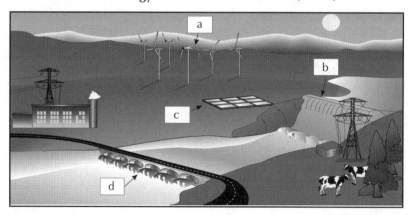

Q5 **List <u>two</u> advantages and <u>two</u> disadvantages of nuclear power.**

Acid Rain

Q1   Answer the following questions:

    a)   What is acid rain?

    b)   How do power stations contribute to acid rain?

Q2   Copy and complete this passage by filling in the spaces with the correct words.

    Acid rain is a weak solution of _____ and nitric acids.

    It forms when chemicals mix with_____ in the atmosphere.

    Factories use high _____ to disperse gases, so acid rain may

    travel a long _____ before it is deposited.

    Chemicals from England can fall in Scotland and Sweden because of the

    _____ .

Q3   Decide whether each of the sentences about acid rain below is true or false.
Write out the true sentences.

    a)   Acid rain makes rivers and lakes too acidic for fish.

    b)   Acid rain dissolves limestone and damages buildings.

    c)   Acid rain is caused by coal mining.

    d)   Acid rain removes vital nutrients from the soil.

Q4   Describe how the methods shown in the diagrams can be used to reduce acid rain.

a)

b)

c)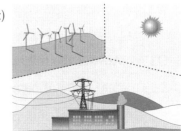

Global Warming

Q1 **Look at the diagram below.**
Copy and complete the sentences to show the causes of global warming.

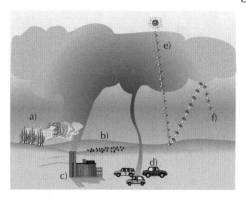

a) Burning wood as fuel releases the gases _____ _____ and
_____ into the air.

b) Cleared areas no longer use up the gas _____ _____ in
_____.

c) The burning of _____ _____ releases
_____ _____ into the air.

d) Cars burn _____ _____ too.

e) The sun's rays can pass through the _____ and warm the earth.

f) But heat from the earth can't escape through the pollution,
and so the Earth's _____ rises.

Q2 **Match the phrases below to make four sentences that describe**
why there is conflict over reducing global warming.

LEDCs burn fossil fuels...	... to sell their oil overseas.
Oil producing countries want...	...to develop their industries.
People want to drive cars...	...to maintain their living standard.
The MEDCs are keen...	...to save time and maintain their independence.

Q3 **Answer the following questions about the effects of global warming:**

a) What is happening to the polar ice? Why is this a concern?

b) Name <u>four</u> places that will be affected by the process you described in a).

c) What could happen to the climate in the UK if
the flow of the North Atlantic Drift is altered.

Q1 Look at these comments from members of a family living in the UK. Write a paragraph explaining how this family contributes to air, land and water pollution.

Rosie, 13: "It's my turn to put the bin out this week."

Jim, 39: "The electricity bill was really high this month."

Jan, 40: "Babies create so much washing and cleaning."

Roger, 17: "I need my own car now I've passed my driving test."

Q2 Pollution can have serious affects on people, wildlife and the environment.
This article describes the effects of oil pollution.

How much does oil really cost?

Oil tankers sometimes spill their cargo in stormy weather or high seas. For example, the Braer ran aground off the Shetland Islands in January 1993. Oil blowing off the sea contaminated wildlife, pastures and crops. Farmers hoped to be compensated for damaged crops and lost income. Local wildlife suffered — birds' feathers became coated in oil, making it difficult for them to stay warm. The birds ingested the oil when preening. As a result many birds died. Animals such as otters also ingested oil.

In Nigeria oil has spilt onto farmland destroying food. Gas flaring releases poisonous fumes. These fumes damage the health of local people. Oil also gets into local water supplies causing diarrhoea and vomiting.

Make a table which has two columns — one for the harmful effects of oil on people, and one for the harmful effects of oil on wildlife and the environment. Complete the table by putting the phrases that have been underlined in the article into the right columns.

Q3 Pollution is a worldwide problem because it can be created in one part of the world and affect other places. Give an example of pollution that has affected more than one country.

The Leisure Industry

Q1   Write a paragraph to explain why the leisure industry is growing.
Don't forget to mention wages and working hours in your answer.

Q2   Give two examples of 'new' leisure activities.

Q3   Explain how each of the following is helping the leisure industry to expand:

    a)   Paid holidays

    b)   Cheaper air travel

    c)   Disposable incomes

    d)   Jet aircraft

Q4   Look at the pie charts below.

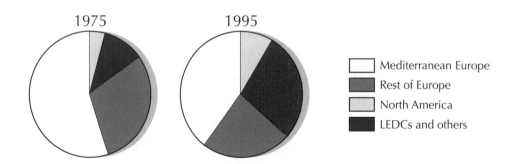

    a)   Which area showed the biggest increase in the destination of
British holiday makers between 1975 and 1995?

    b)   Give <u>two</u> reasons why people can travel to these places more easily than in 1975.

    c)   Give <u>two</u> reasons why unusual tourist destinations are increasingly popular.

Q1 Complete the passage below about tourism in LEDCs using the words in the box.

Tourism brings _____ money into LEDCs. There is new

_____ by big companies in hotels and _____.

New _____ are created for _____ people.

Local _____ are strengthened.

The country's infrastructure is _____.

Other industries _____ into the area.

Local _____ is available and costs are still _____.

airports	foreign	investment	labour	jobs
cheap	businesses	local	developed	move

Q2 Give <u>three</u> disadvantages of tourism in LEDCs.

Q3 In recent years game parks have become popular holiday destinations.

a) What are game parks?

b) Name one example of a game park and say what country it is in.

Q4 Answer these questions:

a) Explain what ecotourism is.

b) Give <u>three</u> ways in which ecotourism aims to be sustainable.

c) Look at the photos below. Do you think they show sustainable
or unsustainable activities in LEDCs? Explain your answers.

i)

Logging to make
room for a new hotel.

ii)

Educational dives to promote
understanding of coral reefs.

Tourism and Conflict

Q1 Tourism depends on human and natural resources.
Put these words into two columns: human and natural.

warm sunshine   **culture**   **mountains**   **beaches**   **art**   **snow**   **architecture**

Q2 Match each of the tourist demands a) - e) with the potential conflict i) - v).

a) Tourists need communication routes so they can get to the places they want to visit.

b) Tourists expect to see unspoilt landscapes, not industrial sites.

c) Tourists expect to see 'old-fashioned' facilities.

d) Tourists expect to walk across farmland undisturbed.

e) Some tourists expect peace and quiet in the countryside.

i) Some residents want up-to-date facilities like supermarkets and shopping centres.

ii) Industries providing jobs often spoil the natural landscape.

iii) Farmers keep tourists off their land because they need it for agriculture.

iv) Roads and tourist facilities are often built on farmland and open space.

v) Other tourists like to pursue noisy activities like water-skiing.

Q3 There are often cultural differences between MEDCs and LEDCs.

a) Explain why the actions of the people in the photo may cause conflict in an LEDC.

b) Are the following statements true or false?

i) People in LEDCs often copy the tourists' style of clothes.

ii) Tourism cannot harm indigenous cultures.

iii) Tourists from MEDCs often demand Western-style drinks and menus.

iv) Many MEDC tourists don't bother to learn the language of the LEDCs they visit.

Q1   Copy and complete this sentence using the correct words from the pairs:

The 25% of the world's population who live in
(MEDCs / LEDCs) own **(80% / 50%)** of the world's wealth.

Q2   Geographers use special terms to describe richer and poorer countries.

a) What does MEDC stand for?

b) Briefly explain what MEDCs are.

c) Name two examples of MEDCs.

Q3   What term do geographers use to describe the world's poorer countries?

Q4   Explain what is meant by the term 'development gap'. How is it usually measured?

Q5   Write out this paragraph, choosing words from the box to fill in the spaces.

The _____-South Divide separates developed from developing countries.
The _____ countries are all in the northern _____,
except for Australia and_____. Poor countries are mostly in the tropics
and the _____ hemisphere.

southern	developing	Japan
New Zealand	North	hemisphere
West	area	developed

Q6   Describe <u>three</u> factors that cause some countries to be poor and some to be rich.

Q1 What is a country's Gross National Product? What does it measure?

Q2 Copy and complete the table to show what these terms mean:

Term	Meaning
Life expectancy	
Infant mortality rate	
Calorie intake	
Energy consumption	
Literacy rate	

Q3 Copy out these sentences, choosing the correct answers from the pairs.

a) In Ethiopia the life expectancy for women is **(48 / 67)** years.

b) In the UK, **(15% / 80%)** of the total population live in towns and cities.

c) In Ethiopia, **(60% / 36%)** of all adults can read.

d) In the UK the GNP per capita is **($28,700 / $11,300)** per year.

e) In Ethiopia the average calorie intake is **(3317 / 1610)** per day.

Q4 Look at the scatter-graph below then answer the questions underneath.

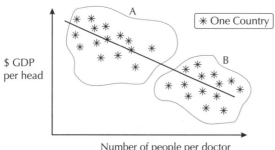

a) Are the countries in group A MEDCs or LEDCs?

b) Explain what the graph tells us about facilities in MEDCs and LEDCs.

Q5 Why can it be difficult to compare countries using indices?

Q1 Look at the map. Name the natural hazards that are a problem in the places listed below it (there may be more than one for each place).

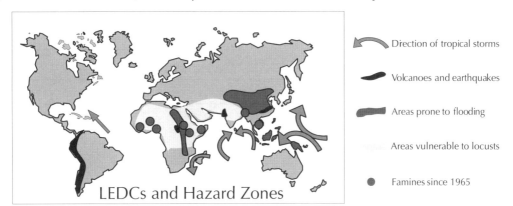

Direction of tropical storms

Volcanoes and earthquakes

Areas prone to flooding

Areas vulnerable to locusts

Famines since 1965

LEDCs and Hazard Zones

    a) West Africa

    b) India

    c) The Caribbean

    d) China

Q2 Copy the passage using the correct options from the pairs.

Large continental land masses have **(extreme / temperate)** climates and interiors are very **(hot / cold)** with long **(monsoon / dry)** seasons. **(Electricity / Water)** supply is a problem and soil **(erosion / deposition)** is a constant threat to **(manufacturing / farming)**. In parts of Asia, the winds bring heavy **(monsoons / mists)**, which cause **(earthquakes / flooding)**.

Q3 Give two alternative names for tropical storms.

Q4 What causes each of these diseases?
    a) Malaria

    b) Kwashiorkor

    c) Typhoid

Q5 What problems do locusts cause?

Water Demand and Supply

Q1 Copy out the sentences and fill in the spaces with the correct words:

a) During winter in the UK, the demand for water is _____ than the supply.

b) During summer in the UK, the demand for water is _____ than the supply.

c) Rainfall is heaviest in the _____ and _____ of the UK, but the demand is highest in the _____ and

_____.

Q2 Match the numbers below to the correct statements from a) - e).

two billion   80   2000   40   2025

a) The amount of people with no water supply in 1995.

b) The percentage of diseases that are caused by a lack of clean water in LEDCs.

c) The amount of people with access to sanitation (sinks and toilets).

d) The year of a severe drought in SE Ethiopia.

e) By this year, two thirds of the world's population won't have access to clean water.

Q3 Describe how each of the following can improve the water situation in LEDCs:

a) Sprays and drip feeding of crops

b) Self-help schemes

c) Concrete lining of wells

d) Education

Q4 The Aswan Dam was built in the upper reaches of the River Nile in the 1960s to try and solve some of Egypt's water shortage problems. Make a table to show five advantages and five disadvantages of building the Aswan Dam.

International Trade

Q1 Relying on primary goods causes four main problems for LEDCs.
Describe why each of the following causes problems:

 a) The value of raw materials

 b) MEDCs decide prices

 c) Fluctuation of prices

 d) Man-made alternatives to raw materials

Q2 Name four products that are typical exports from

 a) LEDCs

 b) Britain

Q3 What does the graph below tell you about the prices of goods produced in MEDCs
and LEDCs? What consequences do these trends have for the countries' economies?

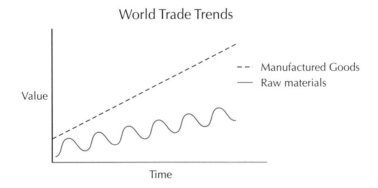

Q4 Answer the following questions:

 a) Explain what a trade bloc is.

 b) Give <u>two</u> examples of trade blocs.

 c) Why do trade blocs disadvantage LEDCs?

 d) Explain how countries within a trade bloc encourage trade with each other.

Development Projects

Q1   Write a definition of 'development projects'.

Q2   Explain the difference between large scale prestige projects and small scale projects.

Q3   Give <u>three</u> advantages of small scale projects.

Q4   How do each of the following create problems with prestige projects in LEDCs?

      a)   Money must be borrowed from MEDCs.

      b)   Expertise and technology is provided by MEDCs.

      c)   Infrastructures are not well-developed.

      d)   Fuel and maintenance for new machinery is unavailable.

Q5   Answer these questions about small scale projects:

      a)   How are small-scale projects funded?

      b)   How do self-help projects help local people to become self-sufficient?

Q6   There are three main categories of self-help schemes.
      For each category, give two examples of the kind of project they might involve:

      a)   Provision of basic necessities

      b)   Provision of essential services

      c)   Low cost borrowing and saving schemes

Q1   **Explain what is meant by 'appropriate technology'.**

Q2   **Match the terms a) - d) with the correct explanations from i) - iv)**

    a)   Appropriate technology must be affordable.

    b)   It must be sustainable.

    c)   It must be right for the place.

    d)   It must be right for the people.

    i)   The project should be run by local people with little outside help.

    ii)   The initial cost and maintenance must be cheap enough for people to afford.

    iii)   It must provide long-term use for people with little impact on the environment.

    iv)   Local technology and expertise should be used whenever possible.

Q3   **Explain what 'fair trade' means.**

Q4   **Choose <u>three</u> of the following phrases to describe producers who follow the 'fair trade' rules.**

    a) exploit their workers

    b) pay low prices for goods

    c) use child labour

    d) help the environment

    e) appeal to 'ethical' shoppers

    f) work long hours

    g) pay a fair wage

    h) have poor standards of safety

Q5   **Give <u>three</u> examples of organisations who obey the 'Fair Trade Rules'.**

The Question of Aid

Q1 **Copy out this paragraph about aid, using the correct options from the pairs.**

Aid is the giving of **(resources / responsibilities)** from one country to another.
It is usually given from **(more / less)** economically developed countries to
(more / less) economically developed countries.

Q2 **Explain what is meant by these terms:**

a) bilateral aid

b) multilateral aid

c) non-governmental aid

d) tied aid

Q3 **Explain the difference between the <u>short-term</u> and <u>long-term</u> aid.**

Q4 **Write down whether each of these quotes is a reason <u>for</u> or a reason <u>against</u> giving aid.**

a) Aid is spent on prestige projects instead of on real needs. Anyway, the profits from prestige projects go to MEDCs, not needy people in LEDCs.

b) Aid to provide things like clean water and better agricultural machinery means that in the future people in the third world will be able to escape from the need to live off aid.

c) Aid is used to exert political pressure. Nobody ever gives aid purely to help others — there are always conditions attached.

d) Aid increases dependency of LEDCs on donor countries — it makes people expect to have the standard of living that people in MEDCs have. Unfortunately, that's unrealistic.

Ordnance Survey Maps

Q1 Look at this map of part of the Isle of Wight. Imagine you are going on holiday to the Isle of Wight. The ferry docks in Yarmouth (grid reference 354898). You plan to camp at grid reference 335879.

© Crown copyright, License no. 100034841

1 cm = 1 km

Now answer these questions:

a) What main road will you travel on to get to the campsite?

b) In what directions will you be travelling?

c) How far will you travel on this road before you turn south at the crossroads (grid reference 336881)? Write your answer in kilometres and metres.

d) When you arrive, the campsite is full.

Give a 6 figure grid reference for an alternative campsite on the island.

Q2 You decide to send a postcard to your friend. Copy the paragraph below and fill in the gaps. The words and phrases in brackets tell you what type of information needs to go in the gaps.

Dear Anne,

Having a great time! We have visited Tennyson's Monument _____ (**4 figure grid reference**) and Fort Victoria Country Park _____ (**4 figure grid reference**). Yesterday we went for a walk. We parked at grid reference 324856 and walked _____ (**compass direction**) towards Pleasure Park. Then we walked back to the car park, first along the _____ (**name of a B road**), then along two smaller roads, past a place called Nodewell Farm. The walk was _____ (**distance in kilometres and metres**) long. From Jane.

Ordnance Survey Maps

Q1 **Look at this map of Leyburn. Then answer the questions underneath it.**

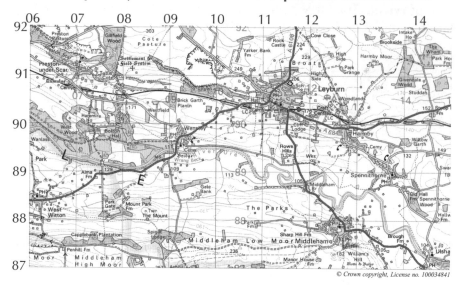

© Crown copyright, License no. 100034841

    a)   Which one of these two squares contains the highest point — 1390 or 1191?

    b)   Which one of these two squares has the steepest slope — 1288 or 0788?

    c)   If you walked along the footpath from 089896 to 061902,
         would you be going uphill or downhill?

    d)   If you walked along the road from 090893 to 092880,
         would you be going uphill or downhill?

Q2 **Find these three buildings on the map then answer the questions below:**
Gale Bank — 096885, Harmby Moor House — 133912, and Brough Farm — 141876.

    a)   Which building is on a north-facing slope?

    b)   Which building is most likely to flood?

Q3 **Make a large copy of the grid below and use it to draw a sketch map showing the**
site and situation of Leyburn. Draw a 'blob' for Leyburn, and include:

    a)   the main A roads

    b)   the railway

    c)   the river

    d)   shade in the land above 110 metres

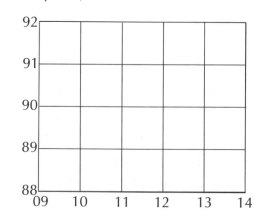

Don't forget to include a title
and compass direction.

Q1 Look at the plan of the University and Brayford Pool area of Lincoln and the photograph. Then answer the questions underneath.

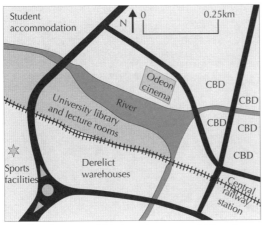

Sketch map of University area of Lincoln

a) In which direction was the camera pointing when the photo was taken?

b) Find the student accommodation on the plan.

Using the plan give three advantages of living in this accommodation.

Q2 Look at the photo of the residential area and the two street plans then answer the questions.

A

B

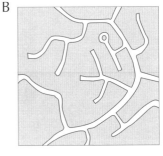

a) Which street plan, A or B, best matches the residential area on the photo?

b) Using the photo and the plan give <u>three</u> disadvantages of living in this area.

Describing Maps and Charts

Q1 Look at the sketch maps below and the list of words.
Write down which word best describes the distribution on each map.

regular   radial   clustered   random   linear

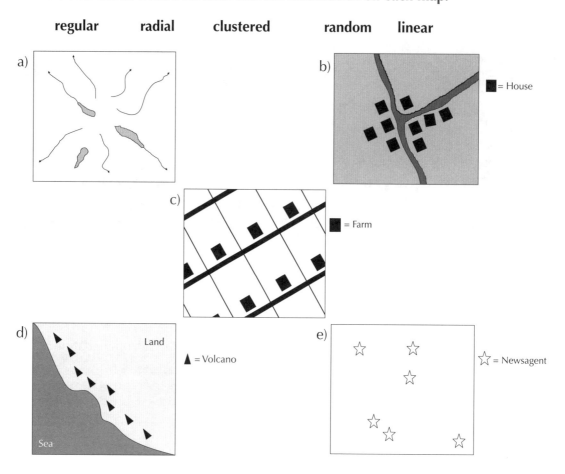

Q2 Look at this photograph of a building next to a waterway in an inner city.

a) Describe the building in the photo.

b) Buildings like the one in the photo are often redeveloped.
How could this building be redeveloped and used in the future?

c) What name is given to the redevelopment of run-down buildings?

Types of Graphs and Charts

Q1 The bar graph shows the environmental quality for two different housing areas in a town. Look carefully at the graph and key.

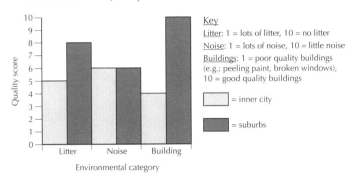

Environmental Quality in Two Residential Areas in a Town

Key
Litter: 1 = lots of litter, 10 = no litter
Noise: 1 = lots of noise, 10 = little noise
Buildings: 1 = poor quality buildings (e.g.; peeling paint, broken windows), 10 = good quality buildings

☐ = inner city

⬛ = suburbs

a) What is the total environmental quality score for the inner city area?

b) Draw a bar graph for a nearby village which has the following environmental scores: litter = 8, noise = 8, housing = 10.

c) Which residential area is the village most similar to?

Q2 Look at the graphs showing the discharge of two different rivers below.
Give <u>two</u> differences and <u>two similarities between them</u>

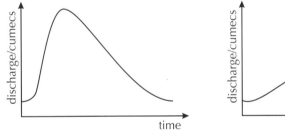
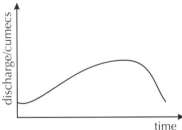

Q3 Draw a <u>line graph</u> showing the changes in the birth rate in the UK using the following data:

Birth rate data for the UK 1760 - 1960

Year	1760	1780	1800	1820	1840	1860	1880	1900	1920	1940	1960
Birth rate	36	37	37	36	32	35	35	29	20	15	14

Q4 Use your line graph to answer these questions:

a) Describe the pattern on the graph.

b) Child labour in factories was banned in the UK in 1833. Use the graph to suggest what effect this had on the birth rate. Give a reason for your answer.

Types of Graphs and Charts

Q1 Look at the pie chart below.
It shows the percentage of land taken up by different land uses in Doncaster's CBD.

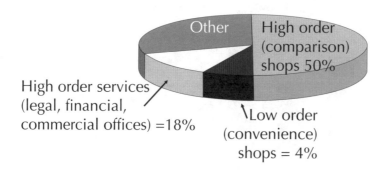

a) Which land use takes up the least area?

b) What is the total percentage of land covered by
high order shops and high order services?

c) What activities and land uses might be included in the 'other' category?
Give <u>three</u> examples.

Q2 A survey was carried out to find out why people were in Doncaster's CBD.
The results were: shopping – 65%, work – 20%, leisure – 15%.
Make a pie chart which shows the results of the survey.

Q3 Read this information about an island called McCallum.

> McCallum has a small agricultural economy concentrating on sheep farming.
>
> Most of the island's income comes from the large tourist economy.
>
> The tourists travel to the island to enjoy the beautiful mountain and coastal scenery.

Look at the triangular graphs below. They show the types of industry making up the
incomes of two islands. Which graph, A or B, is most likely to represent McCallum?

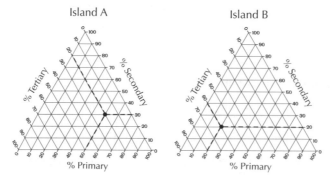

Q1 Look at the topological map. It shows the road pattern on McCallum.
Then answer the questions below it.

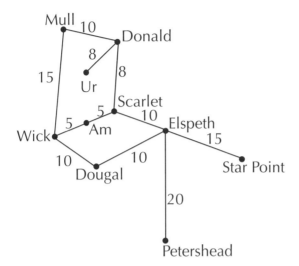

a) How far is it from Ur to Mull by the shortest possible route? (All distances are in km.)

b) Is there a direct route from Dougal to Scarlet?

c) You live at Wick and want to travel to Scarlet. The road from Am to Scarlet is shut.
What is the shortest possible route between Wick and Scarlet?

Q2 Look at the diagrams below. They show the methods people
use to travel home from the CBD in two different towns.

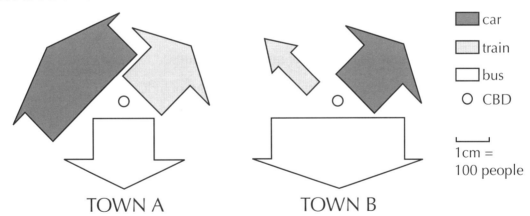

	car
	train
	bus
○	CBD

1cm =
100 people

TOWN A   TOWN B

Now answer these questions:

a) How many people use cars to travel from the CBD in town A?

b) Which town do you think has a 'park and ride' scheme? Explain your answer.

c) In one of these towns the main station is just a short walk from the CBD.
Suggest which town this might be. Give a reason for your answer.

Types of Graphs and Charts

Q1   The isoline map shows how many people were present in the town centre during a ten minute pedestrian count. Look at the isoline map and the street map of Doncaster's CBD.

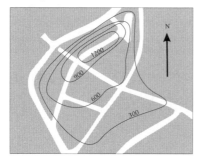   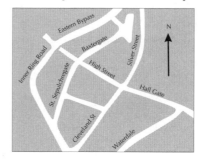

a)   On which street were the most pedestrians counted?

b)   How many pedestrians were there on Hall Gate?

c)   Pedestrian activity decreases very quickly to the north and west of the CBD. Suggest a possible reason for this.

Q2   **Look at the choropleth map below, which shows the world's main climate zones.**

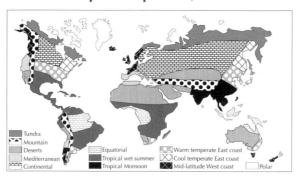

a)   Describe the distribution of Mediterranean climates.

b)   Describe the distribution of mountain climates.

c)   What type of climate does the southern part of India have?

Q3   **Answer the questions below the data table.**

Population and number of services in 10 settlements

Population in thousands	5	15	10	5	10	20	25	10	30	40
Number of services	5	5	10	10	15	20	25	40	40	45

a)   Use the data above to draw a scatter graph showing the relationship between the population size of settlements and the number of services they have. Put the number of services on the horizontal axis, and the population on the vertical axis.

b)   Add a best fit line and circle the anomaly.

c)   What type of correlation does the scatter graph show?